How To Protect And Preserve Your Freedom, Identity And Privacy

Books by Vernon Coleman include:

The Medicine Men (1975)
Paper Doctors (1976)
Stress Control (1978)
The Home Pharmacy (1980)
Aspirin or Ambulance (1980)
Face Values (1981)
The Good Medicine Guide (1982)
Bodypower (1983)
Thomas Winsden's Cricketing Almanack (1983)
Diary of a Cricket Lover (1984)
Bodysense (1984)
Life Without Tranquillisers (1985)
The Story Of Medicine (1985, 1998)
Mindpower (1986)
Addicts and Addictions (1986)
Dr Vernon Coleman's Guide To Alternative Medicine (1988)
Stress Management Techniques (1988)
Know Yourself (1988)
The Health Scandal (1988)
The 20 Minute Health Check (1989)
Sex For Everyone (1989)
Mind Over Body (1989)
Eat Green Lose Weight (1990)
How To Overcome Toxic Stress (1990)
Why Animal Experiments Must Stop (1991)
The Drugs Myth (1992)
Complete Guide To Sex (1993)
How to Conquer Backache (1993)
How to Conquer Pain (1993)
Betrayal of Trust (1994)
Know Your Drugs (1994, 1997)
Food for Thought (1994, revised edition 2000)
The Traditional Home Doctor (1994)
People Watching (1995)
Relief from IBS (1995)

The Parent's Handbook (1995)
Men in Dresses (1996)
Power over Cancer (1996)
Crossdressing (1996)
How to Conquer Arthritis (1996)
High Blood Pressure (1996)
How To Stop Your Doctor Killing You (1996, revised edition 2003)
Fighting For Animals (1996)
Alice and Other Friends (1996)
Spiritpower (1997)
How To Publish Your Own Book (1999)
How To Relax and Overcome Stress (1999)
Animal Rights – Human Wrongs (1999)
Superbody (1999)
Complete Guide to Life (2000)
Strange But True (2000)
Daily Inspirations (2000)
Stomach Problems: Relief At Last (2001)
How To Overcome Guilt (2001)
How To Live Longer (2001)
Sex (2001)
We Love Cats (2002)
England Our England (2002)
Rogue Nation (2003)
People Push Bottles Up Peaceniks (2003)
The Cats' Own Annual (2003)
Confronting The Global Bully (2004)
Saving England (2004)
Why Everything Is Going To Get Worse Before It Gets Better (2004)
The Secret Lives of Cats (2004)
The Cat Basket (2005)
The Truth They Won't Tell You (And Don't Want You To Know) About The EU (2005)
Living in a Fascist Country (2006)
How To Protect And Preserve Your Freedom, Identity And Privacy (2006)

novels
The Village Cricket Tour (1990)
The Bilbury Chronicles (1992)
Bilbury Grange (1993)
Mrs Caldicot's Cabbage War (1993)
Bilbury Revels (1994)
Deadline (1994)
The Man Who Inherited a Golf Course (1995)
Bilbury Pie (1995)
Bilbury Country (1996)
Second Innings (1999)
Around the Wicket (2000)
It's Never Too Late (2001)
Paris In My Springtime (2002)
Mrs Caldicot's Knickerbocker Glory (2003)
Too Many Clubs And Not Enough Balls (2005)
Tunnel (1980, 2005)

as Edward Vernon
Practice Makes Perfect (1977)
Practise What You Preach (1978)
Getting Into Practice (1979)
Aphrodisiacs – An Owner's Manual (1983)

with Alice
Alice's Diary (1989)
Alice's Adventures (1992)

with Donna Antoinette Coleman
How To Conquer Health Problems Between Ages 50 and 120
(2003)
Health Secrets Doctors Share With Their Families (2005)

How To Protect And Preserve Your Freedom, Identity And Privacy

Crucial Security Tips For Personal Survival In The 21st Century

Vernon Coleman

Published by Blue Books, Publishing House, Trinity Place, Barnstaple, Devon EX32 9HG, England.

Reprinted 2006, 2008

ISBN: 1 899726 41 1

A catalogue record for this book is available from the British Library.

Printed by Antony Rowe, Wiltshire

Dedication

To Donna Anoinette Coleman, a Princess who makes freedom worth fighting for.

Preface

You need to take immediate, serious steps to protect your privacy, freedom, identity and wealth. All of these important aspects of your life are under threat, not just from criminals and confidence tricksters but also from the very people who are supposed to care about these things – your Government, your bank and the institutions and professionals you trust to take care of you.

We are all on our own these days. We must take personal responsibility for protecting those vital, fundamental aspects of our lives – freedom, identity and privacy – which we were, in the past, accustomed to take for granted.

This book will tell you what is happening and why you are in danger. More importantly it will tell you what you can – and must – do to protect yourself, your family and your friends.

Vernon Coleman, January 2006

1

If you threw photocopies of your passport and driving licence out with your rubbish you would not be surprised if you found that your identity has been stolen. Such documents should, like credit card bills, unwanted bank statements and other crucial bits of paper, be shredded before being thrown away.

But banks throw out unwanted photocopies in their rubbish. And they, like the Government, will sell your private, confidential information to anyone who will pay for it.

You can be as careful as you like with your own documents, but if you have handed out copies of your documents you will still be vulnerable because of the sloppy, careless way in which banks and other institutions deal with your paperwork. It is the people working for these institutions who betray us, and who expose us to fraud and identity theft.

The people most likely to expose you to fraud and identity theft are civil servants, bureaucrats and the people who work for your bank and insurance company. (Naturally this means that the more bank accounts and insurance policies you hold the greater you are at risk.)

Government Ministers are constantly warning us about the importance of protecting our identity and of how terrorists can use stolen identities to breach the nation's security. But if the Government was working with Al Qaeda they couldn't do a better job of it.

For example, for several years I predicted that the Government would make a profit by selling the information on ID cards to commercial companies which wanted to build up even more complete pictures of the consumers they are targeting. I claimed that the end result would be less not more security – both for nations as well as individuals.

Not surprisingly, the Government dismissed my prediction as nonsense. (Actually 'complete and utter nonsense' were the precise words. It isn't the first time the Government has dismissed my subsequently proven accurate predictions in this way.)

But then, when they were finally put under pressure by journalists, civil servants at the Home Office eventually admitted that the Government *will* sell the information on identity cards. They will sell the information to stores, credit companies, utility companies, banks, insurance companies and...well, just about anyone prepared to pay for it. They might, I suppose, draw the line if Mr Bin Laden wants to buy information. On the other hand they might just put the price up.

It gets worse.

Companies will be able to buy small electronic 'readers' to put into individual stores. The shop assistants in the store will pop your identity card into their 'reader', tap directly into your database and have a search around in it.

And what information will they have access to?

Well, it seems that the sky is the limit.

When pressed for details the Government has admitted that identity cards will contain: details of the individual's next of kin, address, occupation, place of employment, criminal and non-criminal court records, insurance details, blood group, fingerprints, medical records, retinal pattern, DNA profile and national insurance number.

Moreover, by upgrading low-grade information (such as utility bills) the Government is making it easy for crooks to use ordinary, easily obtainable bits of paper to prove they are you. By making too many bits of irrelevant paper important they have made it easy for thieves to steal your identity. Every utility bill you receive is now almost as valuable as your passport. And, since these things are often thrown away or stolen, your identity is greatly at risk. The Government has stolen our liberty and, at the same time, compromised our privacy.

2

The rules introduced by the Government (allegedly to control terrorism and money laundering) have made life unbearably difficult and dangerous for us all. But they have not resulted in the arrest of a single Al Queda terrorist.

3

Banks, brokers and insurance companies all share the information they acquire from you with other banks, brokers and insurance companies. They pass information around and often they sell it. They use associate companies and credit reference agencies and they outsource more and more of their work to other companies in various parts of the world.

So your security then depends upon the level of security provided by all these institutions. Ultimately, your security depends, of course, upon the quality of the weakest part of the network.

There are two ways in which you are likely to be betrayed: through incompetence and dishonesty.

Your security depends on banks and other institutions having computers which cannot be hacked into and staff who are never tempted to sell information for money. You are also dependent on banks and other institutions dealing securely with your information both while they hold it and when they have finished with it.

Sadly, the evidence shows that in all of these areas, your trust is likely to be misplaced.

The people who threaten your security, your identity and your privacy are not terrorists or criminals.

The people who *really* threaten your security, your identity and your privacy are the Government, the police, your bank, your stockbroker, your insurance company, your credit card company, your local council and every other organisation which pretends to have your interests at heart but which is, in reality, more concerned with exploiting confidential information about you for commercial gain than with protecting you.

4

The system which insists that we provide our passports, gas bills and driving licences before we can open accounts has been designed to satisfy the banks' thirst for more information about their customers (to give them control and enable them to sell new products more effectively) and to give the Government (which has access to all that information) more control not over the lawless but over the law-abiding. Information is power.

Today's manipulators need every piece of information they can acquire.

5

Why does the bank want to see two original utility bills, your latest tax bill and a photocopy of your passport when you just want to open an account? When the assistant says that the law requires you to provide these things is she telling you the truth?

Why, if you want to open an account with a stockbroker are you expected to post a bank statement, a utility bill, your latest council tax demand (originals only of course) and a notarised copy of your passport to their offices several hundred miles away? They say it's to prevent crime, money laundering and terrorism. Are they telling the truth? They say they have to demand these things in order to comply with the law. Is that really what the law says?

Why, when you have had an account with your bank for twenty years, do you get a letter from them telling you that if you don't post them your passport or driving licence within fourteen days they will close your account. Worse still, they tell you that if you don't do what they want, they will freeze any money you've got in your account and you won't be able to get at it. And if you haven't got a passport or a driving licence then hard luck that's your problem.

Why do shops want your name and address if you buy a television set – even if you pay with cash? The shop assistant will tell you that it's to help prevent terrorism and crime. That's probably what they were told to say. Is that the truth?

Why must you provide separate proofs of your address and your identity if you want to buy a mobile telephone? Why do some mobile phone shops refuse to sell you a phone unless you produce a letter from your bank confirming that you are who you say you are? Is this really all a result of the September 11th attack on America? Will the nation's security be threatened if you fail to give them what they demand?

6

The bank clerk and the shop assistant probably don't know it, but they are talking phooey. None of these absurd and time-wasting demands have anything whatsoever to do with terrorism, money laundering or crime.

On the contrary, all of these demands are a real threat to your security and to the nation's security.

You are being conned.

These demands are nothing to do with security.

They're all about one thing.

Money.

The Government and the companies who demand all this private information want your secrets not to protect the nation but so that they can sell them. They want power over you (and everyone else).

7

Remember: every time you hand your private information to a bank or a government department you are endangering your privacy, your identity and your safety.

8

Your privacy, freedom, identity and financial security are all inextricably linked. And no one cares as much as you do about protecting these things.

Your Government, your bank and everyone else who pretends to care, are all in the busy of gouging information out of you. You cannot trust them to make any effort to look after the information they've acquired. You have to take responsibility for protecting your identity and your privacy. The information in this book is intended to give you some idea of the ways in which you can do this.

9

We are all vulnerable – physically and financially. But most people don't recognise just how vulnerable they are. And most people don't realise the identity of their real enemies.

So here is the first rule to remember: The major threat to your safety comes not from criminals or terrorists but from your Government and from the institutions and corporations who work for you and whose services you buy. A little paranoia won't do you any harm. The Government and the banks don't give a fig whether your identity is stolen or not. In fact, you will be safer if you treat the authorities (whoever they are) as though they are deliberately making it easy for thieves to steal your identity

10

Your birth certificate is one of the most valuable and private pieces of paper you own. It is fundamental for proving that you are who you say you are. You should look after your birth certificate carefully.

However, if you do lose your birth certificate you can easily get another. You can buy a copy of your birth certificate by post, telephone or fax. You can buy one over the Internet.

Oh, er, there's one other thing.

Anyone else who wants a copy of your birth certificate can

get one the same way. There is no need for them to provide any identification or say why they need the certificate. There will be a small fee, of course, so that the Government can make money out of selling your identity to anyone who wants to buy it.

When the Government introduces its exciting new identity cards it will be possible for terrorists and crooks to get one of those with a birth certificate.

With your birth certificate, for example.

11

Starting with just a birth certificate (and, remember, it's harder to get a GCSE than it is to get a birth certificate) a crook can assume your entire identity. It happens. And, thanks to the Government, it's easy.

With a birth certificate it is possible to obtain a passport, driving licence and National Insurance number in the name of the person on the birth certificate.

Using the birth certificate the crook applies for a driving licence. He may then apply for a passport. He uses the driving licence as proof of identity when he rents a flat. When he has the flat he has the gas bill, the phone bill, the electricity bill and a place on the electoral roll. In your name. Using your birth date.

He can then open bank accounts, obtain credit cards, apply for state benefits and worse.

All in your name.

What is your Government doing to help prevent this happening?

Er, nothing.

Actually, it's worse than that. Everything they are doing makes you more – not less – vulnerable. Just about every branch of the Government (including the courts) happily sells your information (all those private details which they claim must be kept secret in order to protect the country from terrorists and criminals) and puts everything you thought was confidential into the public domain.

12

A friend of mine says that we should all change our name by deed poll to 'John Prescott', get documentation in that name and then all have ID cards as `John Prescott'. That, he says, would cause merry chaos.

13

The Government gives us all a personal National Insurance number. These numbers are unique. You've got one and I've got one. National Insurance numbers are another vital way of identifying us all. National Insurance numbers are vital for paying tax and for claiming benefits and for proving that you are a genuine citizen. National Insurance numbers are used to prevent tax fraud, benefit fraud and illegal immigration.

The snag is that when all the numbers in circulation were counted the total came to 81 million.

And at that time the population of Britain was 60 million.

If you take the second number away from the first number it leaves 21 million.

(Actually, the second number includes babies and small children who don't have National Insurance numbers but that makes things even worse so don't let's worry about that.)

So, let's say the Government has messed up and given out just 21 million too many National Insurance numbers.

That means that quite a lot of people in Britain have at least two National Insurance numbers.

Or else there's someone out there with 21,000,001 National Insurance numbers.

I just hope he's not a terrorist.

(Actually I'm just being silly. I don't really think that there is one person with 21,000,001 National Insurance numbers. National Insurance numbers are worth £850 each on the black market. So if someone owned all 21,000,000 spares he would be able to sell them for £17,850,000,000 which would make him the richest man in Britain. Not even Cherie Blair could get through that lot. And since the illegal owner of all these National

Insurance numbers would have doubtless set up 21,000,000 separate tax accounts he wouldn't have to pay any tax on the sales – even if he was honest enough to declare it – because each £850 would be comfortably below the tax threshold.)

14

When you apply for a driving licence the Government's agency the Driver and Vehicle Licensing Authority will make absolutely sure that you are who you say you are.

They will demand that you send them acceptable documentation.

What will they accept?

Well, a birth certificate would be nice.

Though they do reserve the right to check on you by insisting that your photograph is signed by someone who says that you are who you say you are.

Ruthless government efficiency again.

Presumably, the DVLA assumes that terrorists and money launderers aren't going to be so devious and dishonest as to sign their own photographs. They wouldn't do that, would they?

15

Passports, as we know them, are a relatively new innovation. The world managed very well without them for thousands of years. And the free movement of people around the world contributed enormously to the growth and development of communities, cities and countries. Marco Polo, Captain Cook, Christopher Columbus and Hannibal all managed quite well without passports.

When passports did exist in previous civilisations they were there for an entirely different purpose. The Chinese almost certainly had passports of some kind. But these weren't designed to restrict the holder in any way. On the contrary, they were medallions or certificates given to a courier as evidence of his bona fides. If an Emperor wanted to send a message he would give his emissary papers or a special medal to show to people who might try to stop him. The document was designed to make sure that people would let him pass.

Modern passports, designed as a means of controlling the movement of citizens, were, I'm afraid, originally conceived by the British. In particular, the aim was to stop lots of people from Africa, India and other outposts of the British Empire coming to England.

But, conscious of the origin of the passport and anxious not to upset its own citizens, the British Government used to print a stern notice on the inside front page of its passports demanding that the holder of the passport be given free passage. It was a strongly worded announcement implying that if anything happened to the holder of the passport then the person responsible would find himself on the wrong end of a British warship. In this way the passport could be used to protect bona fide citizens and to stop outsiders entering the country without authority.

How things have changed.

Today, the passport isn't issued to protect a citizen or a country's borders. Possession of a passport is no longer a right and the holder cannot brandish it with pride. Today, passports are issued to control the movement of citizens. And, as if passports aren't enough, we now also have visas. Hundreds of thousands of people are hired to do nothing but issue passports and visas and to check them. Every year millions of people waste hours and days of their lives queuing up to show their passports, not with pride but with a dull knowledge that the passport is no longer a right or even a privilege but is nothing more than an identity card.

It is perhaps time to ask ourselves (as citizens) whether we need passports any more.

Your passport doesn't offer protection these days and (as thousands of travellers can confirm) no government will do anything to help you if you get into trouble while you are abroad. The politicians you helped elect to look after your interests are too busy pursuing agendas of their own to risk upsetting local politicians by trying to defend you. And the embassy staff who are well-paid to protect the interests of the British people are far too busy choosing the wine which the taxpayer will provide for their next Embassy party to spend time sorting out the problems of travellers who have been foolish enough to get themselves into trouble.

Passports don't protect the country against immigration. If people want to move into a country they will do so illegally if they can't get in legally. Britain is an island and has well-protected ports and airports and yet even the authorities admit that every year hundreds of thousands of people manage to get into the country quite successfully.

Passports don't protect the country from terrorists who want to do it harm. There is a whole industry out there busy making and selling false passports (or stealing and revising existing ones). Terrorists who wish to do a country harm will never ever have any difficulty obtaining whatever pieces of paper they might need to get into it. Passports never stop people who shouldn't be travelling from travelling – and getting into any country they want to get into. Passports merely irritate people, waste time, waste resources and give power to uniformed guards who abuse it.

And although passports are today regarded as the ultimate in identity documents (the father and mother of the identity card) forged copies are becoming ever easier to purchase. In March 2004, it was reported that the going rate for a counterfeit European passport had fallen to £600 (from a previous high of £7,000) and passports were flooding into Britain from factories in Eastern Europe where they were being made to order.

Biometric passports (being brought in by the European Union to please the Americans) will not make any difference to the way terrorists and criminals operate.

Government ministers talk about biometric identification as though they've just cracked the atom and discovered the meaning of life. Biometric identifiers are, of course, as old as people. When you see a friend approaching along the street you use biometric identifiers to help you identify them. Eyes, nose, hair, shape of mouth – all the facial characteristics we use to recognise one another are biometric identifiers. When a relative rings you up you know who is on the other end of the telephone because you recognise their voice. That's another biometric identifier. In the olden days you would have gone into a bank and the teller would have given you cash out of your account because he would have recognised you. Even if you'd had a haircut and worn new lipstick the teller would have still known it was you. These days the chances are that no one in your bank knows you by name. No one can identify you because all the 'personal service' has gone out of banking.

When they are talking about biometric indicators Government ministers are talking about fingerprints and pictures taken by optical scanners. And the half-baked Government ministers who boast about the efficacy of these techniques will usually claim that they are foolproof and will protect you against identity theft.

I suspect that only the really, really hysterically stupid politicians actually believe this. The intelligent ones (er, well there is probably one somewhere but I just can't think of an example) know that machines that measure biometric indicators can be fooled just as easily and as efficiently as any other machine.

Fingerprint scanners rely on tiny amounts of natural grease in your skin forming an image of your fingerprint. Just breathing on some fingerprint scanners will fool them. Alternatively (as anyone who watched a movie made in the last two decades will know) it is possible to have plastic skin made which will give you someone else's fingerprint. Making a prosthetic finger which contains someone else's fingerprint is remarkably easy to do. I'm not going to explain it here because I don't want you to be arrested for being in possession of dangerous material. But, believe me, it's easy to do. And, of course, if you have fingerprints which you find embarrassing, you can burn them off with acid.

Facial recognition systems and iris scanners are also pretty easy to fool. (Much easier than fooling a bank teller who has known you for twenty years.)

16

Britain is awash with identity forgers who are producing birth certificates, National Insurance certificates, driving licences, passports and other documents on a massive scale. Even school children have been involved in some of the forgery ventures. The vast number of illegal immigrants in the country means that there is a constant demand for false driving licences, passports and gas bills.

Not along ago, for example, a couple in London pleaded guilty to producing forged documentation. They had produced over 2,600 false identities and were in possession of 13,000 blank identity documents. Their little factory was equipped with card manufacturing equipment, a plastic card printer and embosser, card readers, a top of the range industrial colour laser printer, four computer systems, laminators, scanners, bank stamps, Immigration and Home Office stamps and Nigerian visa and passport renewal stamps. There were also filing cabinets filled with blank National Insurance cards.

The police raided this identity factory but the authorities don't always like to get involved in these cases, which can be extremely complicated and time consuming.

17

When identity cards have been introduced, the easiest way for a thief to steal your identity will be to get hold of a copy of your passport and one of your gas bills (easily done because when your bank has finished with them they will probably throw them out unshredded in a black plastic bag) and then just obtain an identity card in your name. Then *his* iris scan and fingerprints will become *your* iris scan and fingerprints.

18

There are many people around who take advantage of our fear, distrust and suspicion to make money.

My office took a telephone call recently from a woman

representing an organisation with an impressive sounding name. It appeared to be an official office handling international domain registrations for the Internet. We were told that someone was trying to register domain names for one of our publishing imprints and that this attempted registration was regarded as 'malicious'. We were warned that by buying the domain name the fraudsters were attempting to misrepresent us to the public. What could we do? Well, the 'official' who was ringing us was giving us the opportunity to buy and register the domain name ourselves – and thereby thwart the would-be criminal.

On checking with the genuine source of domain names we found that the people who had called us had no official authority but were simply flogging domain names.

It was, in short, a marketing ploy. If we had fallen for it we would have ended up with several expensive domain names we didn't want simply to stop a non-existent buyer getting hold of them.

Two days later we received an official looking letter headed 'Bank Transaction Confirmation – Please Retain for your Records'. The e-mail contained details of a transaction for £286.95. I didn't know what the transaction was for. Neither did anyone else in the office. It all seemed very official, with merchants bank ID, transaction ID and a load of jargon including passwords.

There was an address for us to e-mail if we had any questions about the order. We would, of course, have to give our bank details in order to explain why the transaction record was faulty.

And that was the scam.

There was no transaction. There had been no bill for £286.95. The fraudsters just wanted us to send them our bank details. By proving that the fake scam was fake we would enable them to complete a genuine scam.

19

Numerous crooks now take advantage of the fact that the Government (and our financial institutions) frequently demand private and personal information.

So, for example, one recent scam involved letters being sent out on what looked like Inland Revenue headed notepaper. (As though the real Inland Revenue wasn't a big enough scam!) These letters were allegedly sent by the Inspector of Taxes from an office address in Cheltenham but were, in reality, the latest in a seemingly endless series of scams carried out by Nigerian fraudsters.

One of the fraudulent letters sent out (and targeted at British nationals living overseas) stated: 'Regulations require we obtain confirmation from you that you remain Not Ordinarily Resident in the UK in order to continue to pay interest on your accounts without deducting UK tax. Please would you therefore complete the enclosed questionnaire or we will be required to deduct UK tax from any future interest paid.'

The Inland Revenue fraudsters could easily use the bank details and personal details demanded to tap into individual accounts and remove money.

Clever scam.

How many people are going to question the Inland Revenue? How many will dare refuse to send them information?

20

Here's another fraud that is becoming popular.

You hear a knock on the door or a ring on the bell. You go to the door and find a postman standing there. He has a packet for you. It looks interesting. But you have to sign for the packet before the postman will hand it over. And you also have to produce some form of identification. 'A driving licence will do,' says the man who looks like a postman.

You trot off and find your driving licence. The postman looks at it and makes a note of your details. He then hands over the packet. He leaves. Excited you rush back into the house and open the packet. The packet contains junk mail. You throw it into the bin and curse the company which has wasted your time and its money on this expensive and complicated form of mailshot. You forget about it.

A week or a month later you find out that your credit rating has crashed. And when the bailiffs or police turn up at your door to arrest you for fraud you discover that someone has opened credit card accounts, store cards and mobile phone accounts in your name.

The postman wasn't a postman at all. He was a confidence trickster collecting personal information.

It's that easy.

21

Then there is something known as the 'Advance Fee Fraud'. This one is also known as the 419 scam, after a section of the Nigerian criminal code, and it is one of the oldest modern frauds around. But it's still around so it obviously still works. We get several of them every week.

The whole thing starts with an e-mail from a stranger who lives in Africa (often but not always Nigeria) and who has a large amount of cash that he wants to move abroad. His problem is that he needs help from someone in the UK. He needs someone honest – like you. The funds are rightfully and legally his, of course, but he has a technical banking problem. You will get a cut of the proceeds if you help out. The sum of money is usually huge (around £20 million) and your cut will be equally impressive (10% of the sum involved).

If you show any interest in earning this £2 million fee for doing very little you will be asked to provide some cash to help get the whole thing going. It all sounds plausible. You have to open a special account so that there is somewhere to put the £20 million. And a lawyer needs to be retained. The amount they want is minute compared to the £2 million. You are asked to transfer just a few thousand pounds.

That, of course, is the last you ever see of your cash.

A variation on this one is for the crook to send you an e-mail telling you that you have won a large prize in a lottery but must send in some money if you are to claim your prize.

People fall for this one every week.

Why would you win a lottery you hadn't even entered?

22

My favourite variation on this bit of trickery is The Pope John Paul II fraud.

You get an e-mail telling you that Pope John Paul II had a secret account full of money. The caller needs your help in liberating the money. In return you'll get a share of the secret account which is, of course, worth millions.

All you have to do is transfer £2,746 to a bank in Monaco in order to pay the release fees.

23

Then there is something called 'phishing'.

You get an e-mail or a telephone call that appears to come from a bank or a large, well-known Internet site. You are asked to reconfirm your name, account details and passwords. The caller or e-mailer will tell you that there has been some fraudulent activity on the site and that the bank (or company) is merely checking accounts and reassuring customers.

You will be asked to confirm that all is well and that none of your money has been stolen.

You do this.

And then they steal all your money.

24

The Internet has provided fraudsters (the sort who used to practise the 'which-upturned-cup-contains-the-pea' trick) with a whole new range of possibilities. And a massive population of potential victims. Using the Internet means that the tricksters don't have to hire a lookout man or keep peeping over their shoulders for approaching policemen.

One of the most successful modern Internet frauds is something known as 'pharming'. This involves the fraudster setting up a website which looks and sounds very much like a genuine website. But isn't.

Imagine that you want to visit your bank's website.

You use a search engine and head for what looks like the genuine site.

But it isn't.

This is an easy mistake to make because the crooks will have built a website which looks and sounds like a well-known bank or other institution. They will have chosen a convincing domain name and they will have made their site look very much like the bank's real site.

When you get to the site that you think is real but isn't, you will be asked to fill in all sorts of details about yourself. You do this happily, comfortable in the knowledge that the bank's site will be very secure.

Only it isn't the bank's site at all, of course.

And you've just given all your private and personal information to a crook.

Goodbye money. Hello police.

25

Then there are the 'boiler rooms'.

Out of the blue you get a phone call or mailshot from a broker who wants you to buy shares in a company which is about to become very successful. The company is probably small and probably overseas. The company will probably have a very sophisticated looking website too. The company probably does something very complicated. It may, for example, have a magnificent piece of software which everyone in a major industry is going to have to buy. The shares are very cheap but are going to rocket. You could turn your modest nest egg into a small fortune. If you mortgage your house you could become a multimillionaire.

You transfer some money or send a cheque and you buy some shares.

Not surprisingly, the company turns out to be worthless. The broker gets rich but you don't.

You have no chance of getting your money back. You were conned. And even if you complain the police will find that the calls you took came not from London (or some other big English city) but from some distant part of the world.

26

Credit card skimming (aka cloning and credit card surfing) has been an enormous problem for years. You hand your credit card to a waiter in a restaurant. He takes it away and comes back a few moments later with your card and the slip for you to sign. But while the card was out of your sight it was put through a mini card reader called a skimmer which extracted all your details and created a clone. Modern skimmers are smaller than a mobile telephone, easy to purchase, cheap to buy and run and inconspicuous. Before you've got home the crooks will have bought very expensive goods with the clone of your card. Or they will have made numerous calls to premium rate phone numbers which they themselves have set up.

Credit card skimming is common in restaurants but is also popular in petrol stations where the crooked assistant behind the counter will take your card to a machine hidden just out of site (maybe below the level of the counter). He may appear to have trouble getting the machine to read the card.

27

Some waiters and shop assistants are less subtle in the way they collect information from customers.

Alarm bells should ring if, when you have offered a credit card in payment, the waiter or shop assistant takes your card away, returns, says the credit card company have some questions for you and then asks you for your birthdate, address, mother's maiden name and so on.

28

If you are really unlucky thieves will use your credit card by chance. This is known as 'hit and miss' or 'tumble and swap'. The crooks invent credit card numbers which are similar to

31

numbers they know exist. It's hit and miss but eventually they find a number which works. If they've hit on your number then you will be the one who loses the money. If more traders and websites demanded the extra three numbers on the back of credit cards this scam would be almost impossible to run.

29

The cash machine scam is a booming industry.

Crooks attach a mini card reader to cash machines, to petrol stations with automated credit card machines and to the doors into bank lobbies. The card reader sucks all the details off your card and the crooks make a clone and buy as much as they can on your card. Another variation on this is that you put your card into a cash machine and it doesn't come out. A friendly passer-by tells you that the machine is broken. You go away. When you've gone the friendly passer-by pulls on the thin thread coming out of the machine and extracts your card.

30

Identity theft is an increasing problem and sometimes low-tech methods may be used. Your details may be stolen in a mugging or a burglary. Or old bank statements, junk mailings and gas bills may be taken out of your rubbish. The consequences can be devastating.

31

With modification, the hard disk on an iPod can be used to store data from a computer. The employee comes into work with an iPod and takes home vast amounts of corporate data. Many banks have banned employees from bringing mobile telephones and hand-held computers to work but at the time of writing they still haven't caught on to the iPod problem.

32

Someone stands right behind you at a cash machine and watches you key in your pin number. When your card pops out they grab it and run away. Or some friendly soul stands next to you moaning about the weather or the bank. You listen and exchange smiles and he watches you key in your PIN number. An alternative technique is to drop a ten pound note on the floor immediately after you've taken your money from the machine. 'Is that yours?' asks the thief. You look down and see the ten pound note. 'I think you just dropped it,' says the thief. 'Thank you,' you say, bending down to pick up the tenner, even though you're pretty sure it isn't yours. While you are bent over the thief helps himself to your card, which has popped out of the cash machine, and totters off. This is a pretty primitive type of fraud and can be fairly easily avoided by making sure that if someone is standing right behind you (and won't move) you abort your transaction, take your card and walk away. If you have an hour or two to waste you can call the police. (The would-be thief will be long gone by the time PC Plod turns up. Actually, in some parts of the country you and the would-be thief will have probably died of old age before PC Plod's grandson turns up.) If you've been done by the 'tenner on the ground' trick just keep the tenner and go into the bank and tell them to cancel your card. You end up ten pounds ahead and the thief ends up ten pounds down and in possession of a useless piece of plastic worth about 0.0001p.

More sophisticated thieves who target cash machines do so by attaching pieces of equipment to the machine which enable them either to get hold of your card or to make a copy of it. If you see anything odd attached to a cash machine do not use it but tell the bank staff.

One of the oldest tricks is known as the 'Lebanese loop'. A thin piece of plastic is poked into the card slot. This stops the machine reading the card but it also stops the card being ejected. When, after five minutes, you leave, convinced that the machine has broken down, the thief pulls out the piece of plastic and brings your card with it. This seems to me to be a hard and rather pathetic way to earn a dishonest living and reinforces my suspicion that some thieves could probably earn a better living working honestly. There are two other tricks worth mentioning here: the card cleaner and the camera. If you turn up at your bank's cash machine and find an official looking device attached to the machine with the words 'card cleaner' on it do not succumb to the instruction taped to the machine. The instruction will tell you to clean your card before putting it into the cash machine. When you put your card into the cleaner the crooks get to read all the details on your card. And if you see a small camera attached to the cash machine be aware that is probably filming you keying in your PIN number. Crooks also use mobile phones and digital cameras to record PIN numbers being keyed in. The technology, it seems, is all on the side of the crook these days.

The one other thing to watch out for is the entirely fake cash machine. This looks like a normal cash machine but isn't. It just collects cards.

You might think, by the way, that the amount crooks can steal will be limited to your daily limit. This isn't necessarily true. There are two ways around the limit. The first, rather obvious, technique is to use stolen cards just before and just after midnight. This enables the crook to take two days allowance in one visit. Much craftier is the technique known as 'reversal fraud'. In this one the crook puts your card into the cash machine and keys in your PIN number. When he removes the money he takes all the notes in the middle of the wad and leaves the outer notes in the machine. After a moment or two the machine, concerned that you have either been called away or fallen down dead, will suck these notes back into itself so that they are not stolen by a passer by. And the machine, unable to count how many notes it has sucked back in, will then cancel the transaction. The crook can keep doing this until he gets tired or the machine runs out of money.

33

The easiest way for crooks to obtain someone's name and credit card details is to hang around near the counter in a large store and then discreetly follow a customer who has made a purchase. Many customers throw away their receipt without even looking at it – particularly if they have (as many people do) used their card for some relatively small purchase (a couple of magazines or a cup of coffee and a cake for example). In a pathetic attempt to prevent this type of fraud (which only affects customers and banks and doesn't affect the retailer) some stores only print four numbers on their receipts. But there is no cooperation between stores. Some stores print the last four digits. Other stores print the middle block. It isn't difficult for a thief to collect several receipts and put together all the information they need. Never throw away your receipts. Always shred them.

34

Beware of forms which come through the post and which demand personal information from you. One common type of form purports to be from the Inland Revenue. The crook asks you to fill in the form in order to avoid going to prison or because they want to send you a tax refund. The phoney form will demand all sorts of vital information. It may require your passport number, your mother's maiden name, your bank account number, your PIN number and so on. The forms look very convincing.

35

The cashier's cheque fiddle usually involves the sale of some high value item (such as car) through an on-line auction site. You are selling your old banger and an American buyer offers you $10,000 for it. You think this wildly overgenerous since you were expecting to get no more than £50. The buyer tells you that he already has a banker's draft (or cashier's cheque) for $15,000 which he has just received in payment for the car he has sold. He says that he will send you the banker's draft and will trust you to wire him the

$5,000 change once the cheque has cleared. This, he explains, will speed things up. How can you lose? Ah, but you can.

You hand over the car and pay the cheque in. After a couple of days the bank tells you that the funds are available to you. So you think all is well. You have his $15,000 sitting in your account. You feel warm, knowing that this stranger has trusted you like this. Being an honest soul you rush off to Western Union and send him his $5,000 change.

Two weeks later you get a call from the bank to say that you are now $5,000 overdrawn. The money you paid out has gone. But the cheque you paid in has bounced. It's a forgery. And the thief also has your car.

How does this work?

Simple.

The thief relies on the fact that it can take a couple of weeks for a cheque to clear properly. Banks will tell customers that the cheque has gone into their account after two or three days. But in reality the cheque takes longer than that to be cleared.

36

All this is bad enough. But, as I've already pointed out, for most people the biggest threat to their security, identity, privacy and wealth comes not from these relatively petty crooks but from the big ones.

The sad fact is that these days you can't really trust anyone who isn't genuinely close to you. In almost every area of human and commercial endeavour you will find people whose primary purpose in life is to con you, trick you or cheat you in some way.

In a way this is nothing new.

'No lesson seems to be so deeply inculcated by the experience of life as that you should never trust experts. If you believe the doctors, nothing is wholesome; if you believe the theologians, nothing is innocent; if you believe the military, nothing is safe,' said Robert Arthur Talbot Gasgoyne Cecil, the third Marquess of Salisbury. I don't know precisely when he said it but he died in 1903 so it was presumably some time before then.

But things have got worse.

The medical profession is educated, and to a large extent owned, by the pharmaceutical industry. If you find a doctor whom you genuinely trust then you should stick with him (or her) through thick and thin. The real tragedy about the medical profession is that most doctors don't even know (or don't want to know) that what they are telling (and doing to) their patients is simply what the ruthless drug companies want them to tell them (and do to them).

Your chances of finding an honest estate agent are probably as slim as your chances of finding an honourable politician which is to say that it is pretty unlikely. Lawyers – well the less said about them the better except that Shakespeare was probably right.

But it is in the realms of financial advice that the real sharks are basking these days. Investment advisers, brokers, bankers and others can no longer be trusted to do anything other than steal as much as they can from their clients. The advisers who don't actually steal money from you will lose it for you through rank incompetence. The many who lost money in Equitable Life and the zero dividend investment trust disaster will testify that it doesn't really matter whether your money is stolen or simply 'lost'. The end result is the same. And the Government (in the form of the Financial Services Authority) can be relied upon to turn a blind eye both while the stealing or frittering is going on and afterwards when demands for compensation are being made.

The bottom line is: don't trust the pinstripe suited expert working in the City of London or Harley Street any more than you would trust a 'hunt the lady' trickster working off a cardboard box in Oxford Street.

37

Modern banking procedures make it very easy for crooks to take control of your account and to steal your money. Banks make it much easier for crooks to steal from their existing customers than it is for them to open new accounts and steal from the bank.

The crook gets hold of your bank account number (not too

difficult since it is printed on your cheques) and some other small piece of information about you (your address, perhaps – not too difficult to find if you are listed in the telephone book or on the electoral register).

He then writes to your bank and explains that he (you) is (are) moving. He gives his (your) new address.

The bank dutifully sends your new cheque book and credit or debit cards to your new address.

(In the old days the teller would have said 'Oh, I see you're moving to Auckland! We will miss you.' You would have had a fit and the fraud would have been spotted.)

The crook then quietly empties your account.

And, if you are a good customer, he will run up a nice big overdraft too.

You don't notice any of this because your bank statements have all gone to your new address and so you haven't seen them.

You will (not unreasonably) have assumed either that the bank forgot to post them or that the Post Office lost them.

Your chances of finding the crook are approximately nil. You will, of course, be wasting your time asking the police for help. They are all too busy changing the film in the speed cameras.

38

Like many English people with a home in France I kept a bank account there so that I could pay the rates, the local taxes, the agent, the electricity company, the gas company and so on without having to rush around paying bills with fistfuls of francs.

The true story which follows is a warning; showing just how easy (and confusing) bank fraud can be.

Having once been told that anyone who goes overdrawn in France becomes a serious public enemy, and gets hunted down by pistol toting SWAT teams, I made sure that the account remained in credit. At the beginning of every year I sent the French bank a cheque to cover the bills for the next twelve months.

One January I sent, as was my custom, a cheque for 30,000 FRF to the bank in France. The letter which accompanied the payment was typed and to the cheque I attached a visiting card on which I had written 'thank you very much' in French. I always type letters because after working as a doctor for ten years my handwriting is often illegible. Having given the account its annual feed I thought no more about it.

And then, in late February that same year, I received two documents from the French bank. The first was a bank statement telling me that I had a healthy 60,924 FRF in my account. The second, a most mysterious document informed me that 238,000 FRF had been taken out of my account and put into a bank in Monte Carlo. The form even gave me the name and passport number of the account holder in Monte Carlo.

I had never heard of this person and my first thought was that this was some sort of error. Banks do make mistakes from time to time and this transaction seemed so outrageous and bizarre that I could only assume that the computer had sent me someone else's details by mistake.

Nevertheless, I was alarmed by this odd document – and by the fact that if the transaction really had gone through I would by now be considerably overdrawn. I sent a fax to the bank asking them to let me know what was going on.

Much to my astonishment (and my horror) the bank responded by sending me a copy of a letter which, they claimed, contained both my instructions and my authority for the transfer. My confusion was compounded by the fact that the letter authorising the removal of 238,000 FRF from my account had apparently been accompanied by a cheque (from someone of whom I had never heard) putting 176,232.77 FRF into my account. This cheque came from another branch of the same bank. The money going out of my account had left almost the moment the money coming in had arrived. Indeed, the cheque had apparently been cleared almost instantaneously – without any of the delays one normally associates with banks these days.

The letter they sent me hadn't been written by me and it was pretty obviously a forgery. The forger understood how French banks work but he (or she) wasn't a terribly good forger. He or she had made several fairly fundamental errors.

First, the handwriting looked absolutely nothing like mine.

Second, the signature was nothing like mine either. There was a huge gap between my two names – presumably where the forger had stopped for a breather.

Third, the letter was written in what appeared to me to be perfect French. (The French was so perfect that I had to use a dictionary to find out what some of the words meant. I try hard but foreign languages aren't my strong point and after nearly half a century of trying hard my French is still unmistakably English. Everyone to whom I have ever spoken at the bank would know that to say that my French is poor would be generous.)

The forger had written my address on the letter I was supposed to have written. But he had carelessly mis-spelt the name of the town where I lived. If the letter had been typed it would, I suppose, have been conceivable that I might have made such a mistake. But it did seem to me that even a French bank employee might have thought it odd of me to mis-spell the name of my own town when writing it out by hand.

To make things worse the forger had got my address wrong. And he or she had written it in a mixture of French and English.

All things considered this was not a world class forgery.

However, although the forger wasn't too hot on forging he or she was pretty hot on banking procedure and clearly knew a good deal about the way French banks work. He (or she) had given the bank very specific instructions.

The forger had, however, made a number of other errors. He or she had, for example, forgotten to put 'France' in the bank's address – despite the fact that he or she was apparently writing from England. And according to the address written in the top right hand corner the forged letter had allegedly been written in the UK on the 9th February. This was of significance because the bank had put a date stamp on the letter when it had been received. And the date stamp was 10th February.

Now, I lived in a fairly remote part of Devon and when the postal authorities really got their act together it was possible to move a letter from Devon to France in three days. A week to ten days was by no means unusual.

I was, as you can probably imagine, slightly put out by the fact that despite the obvious errors, and the fact that these transactions were thoroughly out of character for the account, no one at the bank had bothered to contact me before sending my money on holiday to Monaco – a pleasant enough area but part of a stretch of coastline which has, in the past, not always been entirely unassociated with some slightly dodgy financial activity.

What made the whole thing even more surprising was the fact that the illegal transaction had made my account overdrawn. I had always thought that being overdrawn in France was regarded as some sort of fairly heinous activity. But this transaction had taken me deeply into the red without anyone at the bank showing much concern. I felt that alarm bells should have been ringing loud enough to waken the dead. But it seemed that no one had noticed anything.

When I sent another fax protesting about what had happened the bank sent me a copy of my visiting card which, they said, had accompanied the forged letter of instruction and which they had regarded as some sort of verification. The visiting card was identical to the card which I had sent to the bank in January. And, oddly enough, the message on the card was identical to the message I had scribbled on the visiting card which I had sent.

I wrote to the manager of the French bank demanding my money back.

But the French bank didn't seem keen to give me the money back. And they didn't even apologise.

A friend who works in a bank (not in France) cheered me up enormously by telling me that if the bank decided that it had acted reasonably in giving away my money I wouldn't get it back. He told me that if a forgery is good enough then it is the customer who loses out. The bank will simply say that it gave away the customer's money in good faith.

I got the feeling that I wasn't going to get anywhere unless I cranked things up a bit.

I wrote out a lengthy statement, detailing exactly what had happened, had it professionally translated so that there would be no errors, and sent copies to the bank, to the Procureur de la

Republique Francaise (who sounds as if he does something slightly dodgy in Montmartre but who, I was assured, has more of an interest in matters legal than in women in red stilettos and fishnet stockings) and to the French banking Ombudsman.

My next thought was, of course, to contact the police.

I'm rather old-fashioned in some ways and although I know it's probably pretty stupid and naive of me the words 'robbery' and 'police' still go together in my mind.

But I didn't much fancy trying to persuade the French police to take an interest. Rightly or wrongly I had the feeling that they wouldn't be terribly interested in the fact that an Englishman had lost money which he had put into a French bank. And the problem was far too complex for me to explain in schoolboy French. I was also slightly concerned about my own legal position. A cheque had arrived in my account from some mysterious source and a not inconsiderable sum of money had gone whizzing off to Monaco. The words 'money' and 'laundering' kept wandering into my mind. I didn't want to wander into a French police station and find myself being arrested for something someone else had done. These things happen.

So, with more optimism than hope, I contacted the local English police station. It had occurred to me that the police might be interested in a forgery and the theft of considerably more than £20,000.

Oh dear.

I telephoned the local police station numerous times and explained the situation to several people. Eventually I got a call back from a duty sergeant who said that all this was outside their jurisdiction and that I should contact a solicitor or a commissioner of oaths with experience in European Law and get him to make a statement on my behalf to the French police.

I told him that I had been under the impression that Interpol had a presence in the UK. The sergeant said that he would make further enquiries and ring me back. Another policeman then told me that Interpol wouldn't be interested because although the money had been allegedly sent from the UK and had eventually found its way to Monaco the crime had taken place in

France. I was getting just a touch frustrated because I'd always had the idea that Interpol existed to deal with exactly this sort of crime.

I telephoned the Interpol Fraud Section in London and spoke to a police officer there. He told me that they *would* deal with the matter but that I had to make a statement through the local police in England. The Interpol officer was the first person in authority who seemed in the slightest bit interested in the fact that over £20,000 had been stolen from my bank account.

I also telephoned the British Embassy in Paris. They said that they couldn't help and that I would have to make a declaration to the police or speak to a lawyer in France who would handle things on my behalf. But they did fax me a list of English speaking French lawyers. (I had by this time decided to continue all my correspondence with the French bank in English. I decided I wanted to be absolutely sure that I understood everything that went on. I didn't have too much difficulty translating their letters to me. But I wanted to be sure that my letters to them said exactly what I wanted them to say.)

After Interpol rang, telling me that the local police had a duty to take a statement from me if I wanted Interpol to help, I telephoned the local Fraud Squad. Eventually a Fraud Squad officer also told me that my local police station had a duty to take a statement from me. I rather suspected that he had been told this by the officer working for Interpol.

And so a few days later I spoke to a policeman from the local police station again. They still weren't all that keen to take a statement from me. An officer told me that it could take eight weeks for my statement to get to the French authorities. While the police thought about my request that they take a statement I telephoned a very expensive lawyer with offices in one of the most expensive parts of Paris and made an appointment to see him a few days later.

I was told that there was now quite a battle going on between Interpol and the Crown Prosecution Service. The argument was over whether or not my statement could be translated and sent to France. One policeman told me that they thought they might be able to find a policeman who had been to France on his holidays and who might be able to translate my statement when he was on night duty and things was fairly quiet. I was then told that because of the problem of finding (and, presumably, paying for a translator) I would have to make a statement in French to a French policeman. I was, however, warned that in France I would not be entitled to an interpreter since I was merely a complainant and not an arrestee. It occurred to me that my best bet might be to chuck a brick through a window in France, get arrested, demand an interpreter and then make a statement.

Eventually the local English police decided that they could take a statement from me and send it to Interpol after all. (This may or may not have been linked to the fact that I had sent a message to the local police station making it clear that if I had not heard within 48 hours that my statement would be going to Interpol and then to France I would make a formal complaint about the police to the Chief Constable, the local MP, the Police Complaints Authority, the Home Secretary and a national newspaper. Subtle stuff.)

The following week I went to Paris and saw the lawyer. He told me that he thought that the bank would argue that the fake signature (which didn't look anything like my signature) was a good enough forgery for them to accept and would, therefore, deny liability. He told me that having a handwriting expert prove that the signature and handwriting were not mine would do no good at all because the bank would simply say that they didn't have a handwriting expert on the staff when the forged letter had arrived. He told me that banks dealt with lots of cheques every day and couldn't be held responsible. He told me that they didn't even look at signatures when the cheques were for less than 100,000 FRF. (This one, I pointed out to him, was for over 200,000 FRF). He told me that he worked for French banks (though not, he said, the one which had given my money away). He told me that I wouldn't stand much chance if I went to court. He didn't seem too excited by my loss and he didn't seem particularly keen to help me. I got the impression he would have been happier if I'd just agreed to write off the loss and forget about it. However, I talked to him for well over an hour (at £200 an hour) and eventually he agreed that his assistant would write to the bank on my behalf.

Feeling rather despondent I went back to England.

A week after having seen the French lawyer, when I still hadn't heard anything, I sent him a fax asking to see a copy of his letter to the bank. I told him that I intended to ask my MEP in Brussels to investigate French banking procedures. I also told him that I thought that other English speaking customers (and I pointed out that there are a good many British property owners in France) should know what had happened to me so that they could understand the dangers they faced by leaving money in a French bank rather than a British bank based in France. I told him that I had spoken to the editors of several newspapers.

I got no reply.

And then, a few days later and quite out of the blue, I received a letter from the manager of the French bank telling me that my missing money was going to be put back into my account. There was no explanation and no apology.

The bank had still not refunded the charges they had made as the result of the fact that my account had gone overdrawn. I sent a sharp letter of complaint demanding that I be reimbursed for these fees. Eventually, I received a new statement showing that my account was now back to the condition it had been in before the forged letter had been received. There was still no apology and no explanation.

It was an odd affair. Who wrote the forged letter? How did it get into the banking system? Who owned the account in Monaco? Whose money was put into my account? I have dozens of questions I'd like answered.

Curiously, I haven't heard a word from Interpol or the French police. But none of this is as odd as the fact that the expensive French lawyer whom I had seen in Paris never contacted me again. He didn't send me a copy of the letter he said his assistant would write to the bank.

And he didn't even send me a bill.

Curious.

39

Finally, another odd thing happened.

I received a telephone call from the bank. They told me that they wanted me to close my account and take my business elsewhere. When I visited the bank I had to watch while they ripped up my chequebook. I was then handed (in cash) the contents of my current account. They insisted that the police had interviewed everyone in the bank and that they knew it wasn't anyone there. The bank said the police believed that a mugger had stolen the mailbag containing my visiting card and had used it to help authenticate the fraud. The police presumably believed that the mugger paid in the cheque which accompanied the visiting card, mugged another postman and obtained a cheque payable to another account at another branch of the same bank and paid that into my account. And then somehow found out how much money I had in my account and then wrote a very sophisticated letter purporting to be from me instructing the bank to move all the money from my account to another account which (like all good muggers) they just happened to have waiting in Monaco.

Oh yeah.

So much more logical than suspecting someone working in the bank.

40

There is another reason we should all be as private as we can be; another reason to protect our identity: the compensation culture.

A decade or so ago it became common in the USA for high earners to protect themselves against litigation by putting their savings and their homes into offshore companies. Some doctors found that the costs of buying insurance were so high that they simply couldn't continue to practice – even though they had never had a claim made against them.

Now, in Britain, things have got far worse.

Compensation litigation is big business and thousands of people have found that it's a good way to earn a living. All you need is something that you can describe as an 'accident', and a wealthy target. Specialist companies have been set up and, with the aid of television advertising, have recruited litigants by the thousand. Usually the claims are modest enough to encourage the targets (or their insurance companies) to settle rather than run up huge costs and waste vast amounts of time fighting the case. The people bringing the legal action don't get much of the money, of course. In many cases the firm representing them take most of the proceeds as their fee.

But these accident claims, although still continuing (and a major cause of the dramatic rise in insurance premiums for people running small businesses) are small beer compared to the money that can be obtained by suing an employee for some perceived grievance. So far most of the big compensation claims have involved government departments (the armed forces, the police, the NHS) or local authorities.

A doctor was awarded £465,000 because she became terrified of needles after accidentally pricking herself. A social worker sued the council for which she worked and claimed that she had been exposed to stress at work. She received £140,000. A mother who tried to commit suicide won £2.8 million from her local ambulance service because it took 26 minutes to arrive. A Scottish police officer was awarded £2,000 after being bitten by his own dog; another received £5,000 for exposure to 'excessive noise levels' while riding a motor cycle. A fraudster received £248,000 after claiming he suffered erectile dysfunction after his foot slipped down an uncovered drain at a shower while he was in jail. A violent criminal received £75,000 after blaming his career on his attendance at a school for children with learning difficulties. The mother of a child who was expelled for taking a knife to school with him received £11,000 in compensation because the incident made her feel anxious. A mortuary technician received £15,000 compensation after developing a morbid fear of death. A British soldier who was injured when he fell from an army lorry as he 'windsurfed' on the tailgate received £75,000 of taxpayers' money.

These days anyone who has a little money is at risk. If you

are an employer, a householder or a car owner you could find yourself on the wrong end of an expensive lawsuit.

An employee who was not given a reference by her former employer sued and was awarded £195,000. She claimed that the employer's failure to give her a reference had 'ruined her career'. A woman received around £500,000 after breaking her ankle tripping over a toddler who was running around inside a furniture store. The owners of the store were rather surprised by the verdict since the toddler who was misbehaving belonged to the woman who broke her ankle. (Why didn't they sue her for allowing her toddler to misbehave? They might have won back their £500,000.) A man who was trying to steal hubcaps won £50,000 and medical expenses when his hand was run over. A robber got stuck in a house for 8 days and sued the houseowner's insurance company claiming that the incident caused him 'undue mental anguish'. The jury awarded him over £350,000. A woman who slipped on a puddle of soft drink on a restaurant floor was awarded £80,000 in damages. The drink was on the floor because the woman who was awarded the damages had thrown it at her boyfriend 30 seconds earlier. A man who was bitten by a dog was awarded £10,000. Fair enough? The dog had been on a chain in the owner's back garden at the time. And the man given the £10,000 had climbed over the fence and shot repeatedly at the dog with a pellet gun. A holidaymaker who was hit by a falling coconut sued her travel agent and accepted an out of court settlement. (An estimated 98% of cases are settled out of court). A woman who was trying to sneak out of the window of a nightclub in order to avoid paying her bill fell and knocked out her two front teeth. She was awarded £9,000 and dental expenses. A woman whose boss told her that he thought she had nice 'waps' was awarded £7.8 million in compensation. A woman whose boss allegedly called her 'a tethered goat' got £100,000 and a woman described by her boss as a 'bit of skirt' received £1,000,000. In America, a woman whose boss thought women 'snippy' received £40,000,000. One of the most astonishing was perhaps the man who bought a Winnebago Motor Home and subsequently received over £1,250,000 in damages and a new motor home. After setting the cruise control at 70 mph he left the driver's seat and went into the back of the Motor Home to make himself a cup of coffee. Not surprisingly, with no one at the wheel, the Motor Home crashed and overturned. The man sued Winnebago because the owner's manual didn't warn that this might happen.

A dinner party guest sued her hostess after grazing her bottom when she fell through a chair. (The chair was said to be defective and the litigant used the Occupiers Liability Act which requires the occupier of a property to take all reasonable care to ensure that visitors are safe when they are on his or her premises). A burglar sued a householder when he caught his trousers on a protruding nail in a garden fence. Another burglar sued when he fell through a skylight which didn't take his weight.

You may be tempted to laugh at this bizarre list of money-hungry morons and the crazy society which gives them money. But don't laugh. Every one of these incidents actually happened.

Solicitors and companies specialising in compensation claims often fight on a no-win, no fee basis. The litigant risks nothing. If there is a successful outcome the solicitor gets paid well and the litigant gets something for nothing.

Naturally, the litigants (and their solicitors) tend to target people who have money. They check out their victims before a case starts because they don't want to get involved in expensive litigation and then find that their victim can't afford to pay anything. It isn't difficult to obtain confidential information about an individual's financial situation these days. If a litigious plaintiff and a hungry solicitor think you've got a little money they'll want it.

And so here is another reason to be private, very private, about what you own. And to make yourself (and your money) as difficult to find as possible.

41

Don't just cut your old credit cards into two neat pieces when you've finished with them. Cutting cards in two is often recommended by banks but it's a really stupid thing to do and anyone working in a bank who still thinks this is an effective way to maintain your credit card security should still be walking around with their mittens on little strings threaded through the sleeves of their coat. Fraudsters (even the stupidest ones) can put the two halves together, read the number and use the card to buy things over the telephone or on the Internet. The sensible solution, not advocated by banks and therefore well worthy of your consideration, is to destroy your old credit cards completely. If you have a powerful cross-cut shredder you might be able to shred your unused cards and turn them into plastic confetti (then divide the bits into two bundles and put them into two black bags of household rubbish). Alternatively, burn your cards on the fire or cut them into tiny tiny pieces and throw the bits into separate rubbish bins. I strongly suggest that you do this even if the card you have finished with has 'expired' and is theoretically useless. All this may sound a lot of trouble. But if you have your credit card or your identity stolen you'll waste a good deal more time putting things straight.

42

If you use a commercial photocopier (for example in a copier shop) you should assume that the copier will keep copies of everything it copies. And do remember to remove your original. Leaving documents in a photocopier is commoner than you'd think.

43

When you go out of your home you should take with you what I call a 'mugger's wallet'. Find an old wallet and put into it some relatively unimportant but impressive looking pieces of plastic which look like credit cards. (My 'mugger's wallet' contains a gold card which gives admission to the casino in Monte Carlo and an even more impressive looking piece of plastic which gives a 10% discount off purchases at a chip shop in Devon.) Add a few currency notes left over from old holidays. Stuff in notes which look impressive but which are low grade and worth relatively little. It should be possible to fill a wallet with an impressive looking wad of currency which is worth less than a tenner. When a mugger demands that you hand over your wallet, this is the one you give him (after a moment or two's judicious hesitation, of course). If you are carrying more than a few pounds, don't put all your cash into one 'real' wallet. Carry several wallets and a money belt if necessary. Keep cash stashed in several different places whenever you leave the house.

44

There is a way to send off money without having a bank account, without giving any of your personal or financial details to anyone and without passing any of the Government's strict money laundering tests. It is to buy a Government sponsored postal order from a Government run post office. Hand over your cash and you get what is in effect a cleared cheque. There is no risk of having your identity compromised. So, if you are buying a product from someone you don't entirely trust (or you want to send money to someone but you don't want them to have your bank details) consider using a postal order. Postal orders are in many ways safer, more secret and cheaper than cheques. They clear quickly and are infinitely better for identity security. I've no doubt that terrorists use them all the time but the Government has clearly not worked this out yet.

45

There is so much credit card fraud these days that retailers are rejecting up to 8% of card-not-present transactions on the assumption that they might be fraudulent. Credit card fraud is costing companies hundreds of millions of pounds and the incidence is rising rapidly. Your bank may well promise that it will take responsibility for your losses, or you may have insurance to cover any losses. But the costs of credit card fraud are rising so much that banks and big companies are finding more and more ways of avoiding what you thought was their responsibility.

I suspect that it won't be long before consumers have to take full responsibility for any criminal use of their cards. So here are some tips worth following:

♦ Keep your cards somewhere safe. I know this sounds obvious but if all the people who leave their wallets and purses sitting on cafe tables or pub counters are morons then there are a lot of morons around.

♦ Shred or burn all receipts when you and the taxman have finished with them. Many of the receipts issued by shops contain card numbers. Sometimes only part of the number is printed. Sometimes the whole number is printed. Either way you should make sure that you discard all your receipts with great care.

♦ Check your credit card statements when you get them. You will almost certainly find that there are some items which you don't understand or recognise. This is because the flowers you bought in Southend are likely to have been billed as a debt to a company called G.H.Askwith Petrol Supplies (Newcastle). If you don't recognise an item on your statement call the card company and put it into dispute. Make sure that you have authorised all the withdrawals. Astonishingly, one bank which allowed an insurance company to take money from a man's credit card without his permission told him that the bank allows traders to take money from credit card accounts even when the customer has not approved of the payment. It is safer to assume that this is usual practice rather than exceptional.

46

Ignore all e-mails warning you of a security problem and asking you to send your credit card details to your bank's e-mail address. Ignore these if they purport to come from the Bank of England and to have the authority of both the Queen and the Pope. Fraudsters are crafty these days. They will not write to you from www.crooksandconmen.fr. Their e-mail address is likely to be something far more convincing.

47

Don't give any information to people who ring you up at home (or at work) and want to give you something, ask you something or sell you something. Don't tell them anything. Don't even say 'hello'. Just put the receiver down.

48

Wherever you go, whatever you buy, people will ask for your name and address. Shops frequently demand these details even if you are buying something with cash. And they often demand this information if you are trying to return something. Why? What's it got to do with them? The truth, of course, is that they want your details so that they get good profiles of all their customers (if they feed your name and address into their computer they will be able to see where you work, how much you earn, where you bank, what your hobbies are, whether your are married, where you go on holiday and so on). Once they have your name and address they can write to you, sell your name and address to other companies and send burglars round when you are on holiday.

There are several ways you can respond when people ask you for your name and address and you don't want to give it.

You can simply refuse to answer, pointing out that your name and address have nothing to do with them. This is likely to result in an argument. In some stores the assistant (who isn't receiving commission and doesn't care whether or not his company makes any money) may refuse to complete the transaction. I once tried to buy a new camera at a major retailer. The half-witted Nazi working as an assistant refused to let me buy the camera without giving all sorts of information – including my name and address. He insisted that I would be unable to buy a camera anywhere without giving the information he demanded. I walked out, went across the road and bought the same camera from a competing retailer. It was cheaper too.

You can ask the assistant for the address and postcode of the shop. When he gives it to you, give him that address and postcode.

I do this surprisingly often. Sometimes the assistant seems confused. Most of the time they are too dim to notice. When they want a name I may give them the name of their own shop. I find that the staff are usually too slow to realise what they are writing down. Or I give them the name of a competing retailer. Something like Mr Curry, 4 The High Street, always works well as long as you make sure that you know the postcode. If you want to be really clever you can be Mr Dixon when you buy from Comet, Mr Comet when you buy from Currys and Mr Curry when you buy from Dixons. A friend of mine bought a piece of equipment from a Dixons store and the conversation went like this (I know because I was with him):

'What's your name?'

'Dixon. A Dixon.'

'And your address?'

'What's the address here?'

'What do you mean 'here'?'

'Where we are now?'

'George, what's the address here?'

George tells him.

'So, what's your address?'

My friend gives him the address of the shop, as supplied by George.

The clerk keys in the shop's own address. 'Thank you.' His computer offers a postcode which he and my friend duly accept.

Or you can just give a false name and address. As long as you aren't using a false name and address in order to commit a fraud (e.g. to obtain something without paying for it) this isn't illegal yet (though by the time you read this, I'm afraid it may well be since the Government has already said it intends to make it illegal to use a false name even when there is no fraud intended). If you give a false address make sure that it is an address which doesn't exist. And if you give a false name make sure that it is a false name. Using the name and address of a friend, or of someone you know, could get you into trouble. Going into the video shop, signing up as Tony Blair of 10 Downing Street and renting the porniest films they've got may sound like a good idea but it's probably not.

If you do this a few times H.Marx of Rose Cottage, Gasworks Lane, London will probably end up receiving mail offering him a string of credit cards. Don't bother with a postcode. The chances are that shop assistant won't be able to find your address in his computer without one but that's his problem. If you want to help him out just tell him it's a new building which the Post Office hasn't got round to coding yet.

Finally, if you want to establish a new identity give your real address but a false name. Smith is a good name.

Having a false name can sometimes be extremely useful. For example, I remember going on a publicity tour a few years ago and visiting Liverpool. At the time I was writing a column in *The Sun* newspaper. The then editor of *The Sun* had printed a story claiming that Liverpool fans had behaved appallingly during the Hillsborough Disaster. Every local TV and radio station I visited was inundated with threatening calls the minute my name was announced. When I went to book in at a hotel afterwards I did do so under a false name. And it didn't seem a terribly good idea to give my home address either.

49

The thirst of banks, finance companies, insurers and other institutions for information is seemingly endless. However many forms you complete, however many gas bills you post off, however many times you photocopy your passport they will always want more. They want every scrap of personal information you possess.

Why do they want so much information?

The answers aren't difficult to find.

Just ask yourself some simple questions. (The answers are in brackets.)

1. Was the demand for information planned and introduced before the first recent terrorism attacks? (Yes.)

2. Do these demands help prevent terrorism? (No.)

3. Do these demands prevent crime? (No.)

4. Do banks make a profit out of this information? (Yes.)

5. Does the Government make a profit out of this information? (Yes.)

6. Does the accumulation of this sort of information enable the Government to keep a closer eye on their citizens? (Yes.)

7. Does the accumulation of this information help the Government maximise its collection of taxes? (Yes.)

8. Have the Government's own policies (such as waging illegal wars in Afghanistan and Iraq) increased the danger to British citizens? (Yes.)

50

Increasing numbers of bank customers are receiving letters from people purporting to represent their bank. The letters demand to see passports, birth certificates and other forms of identification and warn of dire consequences if these aren't sent.

But beware!

Complying with these demands may severely damage your financial health.

The absurd demands now being made by banks of their customers are allegedly done to help fight the war on terrorism and money laundering.

In my view this is nonsense.

The demands for private, confidential information are unlikely to have any effect on criminals or terrorists – who will invariably be able to supply van-loads of false or well-forged papers.

Banks have to satisfy themselves that their customers are who they say they are but banks do not have a licence to persecute their customers with absurd demands for unnecessary paperwork.

I recently received a letter from someone claiming to represent the Bank of Scotland. I was asked to send an original document, such as a birth certificate, driving licence, rent card or current firearm certificate, to prove my identity and was told that this would help the bank fight crime and terrorism. But the letter came from someone I'd never heard of and from an address that was entirely new to me and which I had never seen before on correspondence from the bank. The letter ended with a printed signature. I was asked to send the required private document to another address I'd never heard of.

I wrote back to the bank pointing out that since identity theft is now a major problem I did not want to release any personal documents until I received a signed letter from a senior bank officer who undertook to take personal responsibility for the security and safe return of my document. I also insisted that the bank should confirm that it would make no copies of my document.

I pointed out that my requirements were designed to protect the security of the bank, the nation and myself and added that the careless disposal of unwanted documents by financial institutions was undoubtedly a factor in the spread of identity theft. I explained that the letter purporting to come from the bank had a printed signature, that the address on the letterhead did not match the Bank's address on previous communications and that the address on the ready-paid envelope I was sent bore no relationship to the Bank's address which I already had.

I heard nothing more from the Bank. They didn't close my account. And no bulky men in flak jackets turned up demanding to see my gas bills. I didn't even get a reply from my usual contact at the bank, to whom I had sent a copy of the correspondence. Maybe the letter was a hoax and wasn't from the Bank of Scotland at all. Maybe a terrorist group was collecting birth certificates, driving licences, rent books and firearm certificates.

(In a way these checks can be useful. The letter I received drew my attention to the fact that I wasn't getting a very good deal from my arrangement with the Bank of Scotland. I later closed my accounts with them.)

These alleged identity checks are a dangerous, time wasting nonsense. Thousands of customers of major banks have already been tricked into supplying confidential information. Criminals use the information they obtain (such as passwords) to steal money or to hijack the identities of the people they trick. Fraudulent e-mails, tricking customers into parting with personal details, cost American banks and credit card companies $1.2 billion in 2003.

And there is no reason why crooks won't use the ordinary mail to trick bank customers. Con men don't even need to know for certain that you have an account with a specific bank. If they pretend to represent a major bank and send off 1,000 letters to 1,000 names taken at random there is a good chance that 10% of the individuals targeted will have an account with the bank that has been selected.

My advice: be very wary about sending information to anyone purporting to represent a bank.

51

Here's a letter I frequently send to banks demanding to see private documents. The letter can easily be adapted for other institutions.

'We frequently receive requests for confidential personal information. Due to the fact that private information which is obtained in this way may be used both for identity theft and money laundering (and ultimately for terrorism) we are no longer willing to send such information through the post (where it may be lost) or to people personally not known to us. We have received warnings that crooks are now using fake headed notepaper/e-mail/fax addresses to obtain personal information. We are happy to make identifying documents available for inspection only (no copying) by appointment at a mutually convenient place. We ask that bank staff to whom we show documents should bring documentation proving that they are employees of the bank.'

52

No bank has yet been able to produce any evidence of legislation proving that individuals must provide documents on demand. Banks have to satisfy themselves that their customers are who they say they are. But banks are not obliged to request constant supplies of confidential documentation. Indeed, to do so endangers the nation's security.

53

If you refuse to cooperate with banks (and others) who demand to see private documents there is a risk that you will be reported to the authorities (i.e. to the police). But just what are they going to do?

54

Because opening new bank accounts is difficult I suggest that if you are planning to live abroad for a while you consider keeping your UK accounts open. Put in the minimum amount of cash required to keep the account open and to avoid having to pay charges. Many people who return to Britain find that the absence of gas bills makes it impossible for them to open new bank accounts for several months.

55

The security regime favoured by banks is based on the assumption that certain particulars such as your birth date and your mother's maiden name are known only to a few select members of your family. I am astonished at how many banks still treat these pieces of information as of any value at all. Banks themselves have devalued this sort of vital information by misusing it. Your date of birth and mother's maiden name are public property – and easily available. In the bad old days your local bank would have this information but it would keep it locked in a filing cabinet in the branch vault. Today, your information is kept on file and any bank employee with a pass code can get at it. In any institution thousands of people will have access to personal databanks. Some of these people are bound to be incompetent, disgruntled or dishonest. Punishments have in the past been light because banks don't want to draw attention to problems. My advice is that you never use your mother's maiden name as a security password. Mothers' maiden names have been overused and abused. They are simply not secure. And yet banks still insist on using these as evidence that you are who you say you are. If you have a choice ask them to select other pieces of information. The employees of any bank or other institution who still regard date of birth as a useful form of identification clearly care nothing about your security.

Of course, if you feel imaginative you could perhaps give the bank an alternative birth date or mother's maiden name. As long as you remember what you have chosen I cannot see any problems with this. If the bank insists on having your mother's maiden name as a password tell them it's Schonberg Von Hasslehof if you like. (Unless, of course, your mother's maiden name really is Schonberg Von Hasslehof.) As far as I am aware it is not yet illegal to use a false mother's maiden name in order to protect your own security. But do remember what you've told them. (And don't write it down.)

56

If someone steals money from your account it is up to the financial institution to show that you have acted fraudulently or without care. They will probably put pressure on you to admit that the loss was your fault. If it wasn't then don't give in. If the bank cannot prove that the loss was your fault then any losses resulting from the abuse of your credit card or debit card may be limited. Generally speaking, if your card is stolen or lost you may have to pay up to a maximum of £50. (You should not be responsible for anything that is taken after you have reported the loss or theft). If your card has never been lost, or if it is used without your knowledge for a 'card not present' transaction, then you shouldn't have to pay anything. If thieves use hidden scanners or cameras at a cash machine to record your card details then you shouldn't have to pay anything. If you find that bank staff are unhelpful (heaven forbid) then quote the relevant passages of the banking code which you can find on www.bankingcode.org.uk .If that doesn't work make a complaint to the Financial Ombudsman Service.

57

Don't rely on your signature to protect you from bank fraud. Banks will often 'pass' documents (such as cheques) without ever even looking at the signature. You can probably put a cheque through your account if it is signed Mickey Mouse. Of course, if your name really is Mickey Mouse this won't be difficult or much of a worry to you.

58

I strongly recommend that you always unplug the computer you use for Internet access from the telephone line when you are not using it. You should never, ever leave your computer permanently online. If you do then you are making life terribly easy for crooks. They can enter your computer whenever they like. They can read your letters, access your accounts, break your passwords and use your credit cards to purchase all sorts of devilish entertainments: all at their leisure. And they can ring up in the middle of the night and charge all sorts of horrendous costs to your phone line. You won't know anything about it until you get your next bill. None of this has happened to you so far? Or at least you don't think it has? Good. But I know people who smoke who haven't got lung cancer yet. So, whatever the computer experts suggest, I strongly recommend that you unplug your telephone line from your computer when you aren't actually online and using the Internet.

59

Never use wireless systems (the sort that allows you to use your laptop or some other gadget without having to connect it to a telephone point). Wireless networks make it very easy for outsiders to log into your computer and do whatever they want to do with your files.

60

Don't use the ordinary post for truly sensitive or valuable documents. And don't rely on recorded delivery, registered post or special delivery. Sadly, I'm afraid that in my view the Post Office can no longer be trusted with valuable documents. There are, it seems, an increasing number of crooks delivering or working with mail. Some of them probably got their jobs simply so that they could steal valuable items.

If you think I'm being unfair you should know that not even the Government trusts the Post Office with sensitive documents.

For example, the Passport Office doesn't use the Royal Mail to send out passports but chooses to use a courier. On the back of the envelope in which passports travel are the words: 'If delivered incorrectly please call (freephone number). Do not post in the Royal Mail.' These instructions are printed in red, capital letters.

And the Driver and Vehicle Licensing Agency tells drivers not to send debit card details through the post.

61

Try not to let anyone photocopy your passport or driving licence. If asked say that these documents are not available. Offer something else. Every time you give a copy of your passport (or any other significant personal document) to anyone, you are endangering the security of your own identity and you are putting the nation's security at risk. Any institution or organisation which asks you to post a photocopy of your passport is deliberately and recklessly endangering the nation and putting us all at risk. (This is what I tell anyone who asks me to post a copy of my passport.) If you find yourself in a situation where you really do have to hand over a copy of your passport then I suggest that you insist on faxing it or handing over the copy in person. Most banks and other large organisations will have an office or branch somewhere near to you. And before you hand over the copy of your passport insist that a named employee sign a short document (which you can prepare beforehand) accepting receipt of the document and taking responsibility for its care or destruction.

62

You must weigh up the advantages of spreading your assets between a number of bank accounts and of keeping everything you own in one place. The advantage of having lots of accounts is that if one bank goes bust you won't lose everything. The disadvantage is that the more bank accounts you own the more chances there are of a crook getting hold of your private information. One way to deal with this is, perhaps, to keep your day-to-day dealings separate from your long-term investments. It is your day-to-day financial dealings (credit cards and cheques) which are most likely to produce problems and attract attention from crooks. So don't keep too much money in the account with which you pay your credit card bills.

63

Do remember that a large proportion of fraud related to credit cards occurs when cards are being used abroad. The best defence, of course, is to pay cash.

64

When you buy a TV set the firm to which you give your custom may well write to the TV licensing authorities to let them know about your purchase. You may, as I do, regard this is an outrageous breach of confidence. But that won't stop them doing it. If you don't want to receive unnecessary (and rather threatening) letters from the TV licensing people, pay cash when you next purchase a television set and, as long as you are not having the set delivered, give an imaginary name and address. (Refusing to give your name and address seems to arouse great suspicion among counter staff in some stores and is particularly likely to attract attention when buying a television set.) Refusing to give your real name to shop assistants is not yet illegal in the UK (though I can't promise that it won't be by the time this book comes out − indeed by the time this book comes out this book may be illegal) as long as you don't give a false name in order to evade or intend to evade any responsibilities. As far as I know denying the TV licensing stormtroopers the opportunity to send you threatening mail isn't yet an offence.

65

Make sure that your bank and credit card company have a telephone number for you so that they can ring if there are any emergency problems or queries. When they use your private number to try to sell you a new product (as they doubtless will), explain that the number is for emergencies only, that you were performing delicate brain surgery when they called and that you have had to leave your patient dripping blood and oozing brains in order to take their call. Few things about banks annoy me more than the way that they use private phone numbers, given for emergencies, when they want to sell you a new product. When they can't get through to you the message they leave always sounds important. ('Please ring the bank as soon as possible.') And the result is that if you miss a call on a Friday afternoon you are likely to spend the whole weekend worrying that your accounts are being emptied by crooks. When you finally get through to the caller on Monday morning you find that you are speaking to a salesman wanting to flog you something that no one with half a brain would even bother to waste time sneering at.

66

Take great care when using cash dispensing machines. Use machines which are in well-lit, well-frequented places where you are less likely to be mugged for your money. If possible use machines which are indoors and protected by closed circuit television cameras and bullet headed men having trouble holding back slavering Dobermann pinschers. Try not to use cash machines late at night. If the machine you use looks different in any way tell your bank. Before using the machine run your finger along the card slot and see if you can feel any small protrusions. If there are then there is probably a Lebanese tape loop in the machine – ready to trap your card so that a thief can retrieve it. Always tell your bank if your card isn't ejected at the end of the transaction. Be wary of people standing close to you. If people are too close and don't move back, abort your transaction. Stand close to the machine and shield the keypad with your body. Don't allow yourself to be distracted – even by friendly, decent looking strangers. After completing a transaction put your money and card away immediately. Put your receipt away carefully. When you have checked it against your statement and no longer need it destroy the receipt as carefully as you would any other important document. Finally, remember that you don't have to use a machine; if you have a couple of hours to spare you can always collect some of your cash from a clerk in the bank.

67

There was a time when shopkeepers welcomed cash payments. No more. In most countries it is now illegal to pay more than small bills with hard currency. Try to pay with cash and you may well find that your offer is refused. Even if your cash is accepted the chances are growing that your suspicious behaviour will be reported to the authorities. Cash is no longer king.

Why?

Simple.

People who pay by cash are able to move around relatively anonymously. They don't leave a paper trail of receipts behind them.

The authorities don't like that. They like to know where we all are. Plastic money puts us all in the power of the bureaucrats. They can find us whenever they want to find us. They can see where we've been, where we are and where we are going. They can see what we've spent and what we've spent it on.

All this information is invaluable to tax collectors, of course. And it's also invaluable to companies who want to sell us things and services – and to make money from us.

Cheques will be the next to go. Some banks in Europe have already stopped issuing their customers with cheque books. Once again, the explanation is that cheques make life easier for terrorists. This is nonsense, of course. The fact is that banks can't make much money out of cheques. They have to issue cheque books free of charge. They much prefer credit cards which enable them to charge huge fees – and to keep a computerised eye on their customers' spending habits.

The claim that by stopping us using cash and cheques they are somehow helping to protect us from terrorism is nonsense. Terrorists will still use cash (though they may not shop at the sort of places that are likely to 'shop' them to the authorities). And terrorists will use credit cards without ever having to worry about being traced. They use credit cards in false names and they use stolen credit cards.

And when they want to change cash they (like the money launderers) will use currency change booths (available all over the world) and they will then transport the proceeds by purchasing high value items such as rare postage stamps.

If the authorities don't know this then they are unbelievably incompetent. If they do know, then they know that all the bizarre and intrusive demands they make (two gas bills, a shot gun licence, your passport and so on to withdraw your own money from the bank) are a complete waste of time, designed to bewilder and confuse the vulnerable rather than to stop the malignant terrorist.

68

To commit a 'card not present' fraud all a crook needs is your name, your credit card number and the expiry date. With that information a crook can order as many goods as he likes over the phone or the Internet (until your credit runs out or someone notices that your card is being used in an unusual way).

69

Remember that every time you use a credit card you increase the risk of the card being used fraudulently. Pay cash for small items (such as meals and train tickets) whenever you can. Use your credit card as little as possible. The less you use your card the less likely it is to be misused by someone else. Cash has the advantage of helping you remain private. Airlines and some hotels, restaurants and shops won't accept cash. But cash is still legal tender for most small(ish) purchases. Using cash is also much quicker than using a credit card. (I confess I find myself losing patience with customers who insist on using a credit or debit card to pay for a single magazine in a newsagent's shop.)

70

Be careful how you store old paperwork. You should shred everything that contains information about you unless you really need it. At the very least you should shred unwanted documents which contain bank information, medical information, home address, birth date, application forms (even if only half completed), utility bills and official letters. And if you have old letterheads, with compliments cards or visiting cards that you no longer want you should definitely shred those too.

It would be logical to destroy old accounts and bank statements once you have finished with them. Destroying bank statements, invoices, credit card statements and other bits and pieces of paperwork would save space and improve security enormously. Unfortunately, the Government (which cares nothing for your security or the integrity of your identity) insists that taxpayers keep every scrap of paper for years – thereby putting everyone's security at great risk. For example, if you are a taxpayer you are required by law to keep old accounts way beyond the end of the relevant tax year. If you run a business you will be required to keep vast amounts of old paperwork. Even old insurance policies and paperwork have to be kept in case a former employee or visitor suddenly decides that he wants to sue you because of a fall that occurred years ago

Where do you keep all the stuff?

'Don't keep it where thieves can find it,' advise security experts.

Ha ha. Oh yeah? So just where do they suggest we all hide the boxes of paperwork we are compelled to keep?

Finding enough storage space is one problem. Finding a secure storage space is even harder.

One solution is to rent a lock up storage facility – the sort of place usually rented by people who have excess furniture to store. Such storage facilities are usually very private and relatively cheap.

The sort of people who are likely to break into one of these places are unlikely to be interested in your old accounts – especially if they are hidden under a pile of old, cheap furniture and cardboard boxes full of battered and worthless old books.

71

As long as you don't have to keep it in storage to satisfy the requirements of the Inland Revenue, you should shred anything which has your name on it or which can identity you or which contains anything you don't want printing on a ten foot high advertising hoarding. The best type of shredder is a cross-cut shredder, the sort that cuts paper into tiny pieces rather than long strips. When you empty your shredder give the pieces a good stir to mix them all up and make them all the more difficult to glue back together. And then, when you've put the shreddings into a blackbag, add some kitchen waste to the mixture. Coffee dregs are good for this. If you don't have a shredder, don't have access to a shredder and can't burn documents then tear the delicate parts of sensitive documents into small pieces and put the pieces into different waste bins. Put some in a bin at home, some in a bin at work and some in a bin in the high street.

72

If you decide to save money on a shredder by burning your paperwork be careful. A regular bonfire will do just as well as a shredder as long as you make sure that every piece of paper is properly burnt. Papers have to be burnt singly. If you put a pile of papers onto a bonfire there is a good chance that only the edges will be burnt – leaving the insides perfectly readable. There is also a risk that sheets of blackened paper may rise, whole, into the air and float over your fence and far away. You could end up chasing your old half-burnt bank statements around the neighbourhood.

73

If you put a visiting card or with compliments slip in with a cheque make sure that the card or slip contains the date and details of why it is being used and for whom it is intended, so that it cannot be used in the future by a crook pretending to be you. Don't ever hand out visiting cards without writing the date and the recipient's name on them.

74

One popular trick at the moment is for a crook to ring up and tell people that there has been a mix up with the payment for their electricity. 'You can pay now by credit card,' says the crook. 'Otherwise I'm afraid we have to cut your electricity off tonight.' Appalled, you give your credit card details. You breathe a sigh of relief when the electricity isn't cut off. Three weeks later you discover that someone in Panama has been downloading premium rate paedophile porn from the Internet using your credit card. Three months later, ruined and penniless, you are serving five years in a high security prison where you are being kept in isolation for your own protection.

75

If your bank telephones and wants to talk to you about your account don't give them any personal information until you have proved that they are who they say they are. The easiest way to do this is to tell them that you will ring them back on their main number. Ask them to tell you which department and which employee to ask for. Tell them that you will only ring them via their head office.

76

When giving a password or identification code to a bank or other institution do not give the whole password or code over the telephone. Tell the person at the other end to ask you for three random letters or numbers from the word or code. This helps to protect your security from anyone who can overhear your conversation, or who happens to be tapping your telephone at the time. Banks rarely think of doing this, by the way; it is usually something that you will have to suggest to them. (If banks thought of it they could hide passwords even from their own staff. The staff member would ask you for part of the word or code. They would then key in what you gave them. If it fitted the secure password then all would be well. The transaction would be completed without the bank employee ever knowing or needing to know your entire password.)

77

Never, ever give out information (on the telephone, by fax, through the mail or on the Internet) in response to a 'routine background check'.

78

Thieves who steal your identity data can impersonate you and commit crimes in your name. He or she can open bank accounts (and then borrow money), commit frauds, buy property (with loans taken out in your name), use your existing credit cards and bank accounts, rent property, buy cars, electronic equipment, take holidays, fraudulently obtain social security benefits, redirect your mail. You won't know until it's happened – weeks or months later. You will either get a phone call or letter from a bank demanding repaying. Or creditors will turn up demanding that you return goods you don't have and never had. Or the police will turn up on your doorstep to arrest you.

The Government's silly rules mean that all an ID thief needs are a couple of these:

- your name and address
- your telephone number
- your National Insurance number
- your driving licence number

- account numbers for any of your bank accounts
- credit card numbers
- utility bills
- birth certificate
- passport

All these, you will notice, are the things that banks insist that you hand over to them whenever you want to open an account. And Government departments hold all this information on everyone. They will, of course, sell the information to anyone who wants to buy it.

79

No one seems to have thought about the possibility that ID card 'readers' (the little machines into which your ID card will be put so that the policeman, bureaucrat, customs officer can find out who you are and what size shoes you take) will get into the hands of crooks. But they will. Terrorists, confidence tricksters and others will buy or steal these machines and will use them to 'read' ID cards with absolute ease. How will you know that the man in the uniform who demands to see your ID card is really who he says he is? Unless he carries an ID card which you can put into your 'reader' you'll have to take his word for it. And if you refuse to show him your card and he is a policeman then you'll be guilty of a crime. But if he is a confidence trickster he'll stick your card into his 'reader' and obtain every bit of information about your bank accounts.

80

Perhaps the scariest forms of identity theft is the type that leads to 'multiple application fraud'. This can be really nasty.

One of the worst cases I've heard of involved a retired airforce officer and his wife. The first they knew of their problem was when they got a telephone call from a debt collection agency wanting to know why they were late making payments on an expensive car they had bought.

They knew there was something wrong because they hadn't bought the car the bank had rung about. And they hadn't ever lived where the car had been bought.

Oh dear.

It then turned out that the collection agency had their house under surveillance.

When they saw the credit agreement they had allegedly signed the couple found that the only things correct on the form were their names and social security numbers. Everything else – address, date of birth etc – was false.

The couple then looked at copies of their up-to-date credit reports from three credit reference agencies. To their horror they discovered that the crook (or crooks) had been busy. They'd taken out 33 fraudulent accounts in their names. They had borrowed money, acquired credit cards and bought cars.

Three years later the couple was still trying to clear up the mess – and still copying with the emotional and financial cost of the multiple theft.

This sort of multiple identity fraud is usually conducted by professionals. They will sometimes continue to open new accounts and acquire more credit cards as fast as the victims can close down accounts.

What is your Government doing to prevent this happening?

Er, nothing. Actually, everything they are doing is making it more not less likely.

81

The sooner you spot that you are (or might be) an identity theft victim the more effectively you will be able to deal with it before real damage is done. Amazingly, it takes the average identity theft victim twelve months to realise that they've been 'done'.

Here are some of the warning signs which should alert you to the fact that you might be a victim of identity theft:

1. Your bank statements stop arriving.
2. Other mail you are expecting doesn't arrive.
3. Your home, bag or car is burgled and essential documents

such as your passport, driving licence and bank statements are missing.

4. All or part of your chequebook is missing.

5. Strange expenses which you don't recognise appear on your credit card or bank statement.

6. You receive letters or calls telling you that the application for credit or a mortgage that you haven't made has been accepted or declined. (Both are worrying but, on the balance, the former is more worrying.)

7. The bank tells you that there are suspicious transactions on your account.

8. A credit search in your name shows that you hold accounts you didn't open or that searches have been made which do not relate to enquiries you have made.

9. You find that your credit rating suddenly changes.

10. A debt collector calls or writes and wants money you don't owe.

82

If you are a victim of identity theft you should:

1. Panic. Get it out of your system. Run around yelling 'I've been ruined' for five minutes. You'll feel better. (People who say 'Don't panic!' aren't there, aren't real and have probably never had something awful happen to them.) Then sit down and decide that things could be worse (you could have just had a letter from the hospital telling you that you have twenty minutes to live), that you are going to deal with this and that, if at all possible, you are going to fry the bastard who did it to you. Alternatively, pack a suitcase, change your name and go abroad.

2. Be prepared to spend some time recovering your identity. The authorities estimate that, on average, it takes 300 hours of hard work to repair the damage done by an identity theft. So put aside everything you can. This is going to take over your life for a while. But, again, learning to walk again after an accident can take a lot of time, so keep things in perspective.

3. Establish all the facts. Contact all major credit-reporting agencies to find the extent of the damage.

4. From now on make notes of every phone call you make and every conversation you have. Keep copies of all the letters you write.

5. Report the crime to the police. Get a lawyer. Actually, do these two things the other way round. Don't give the police (or anyone else) original copies of your documentation. Give them copies. If you cannot afford a lawyer, visit your local Citizens Advice Bureau.

6. Contact all the financial institutions with whom you do business. Tell them what has happened.

7. Cancel any credit cards which might be compromised and change any bank account numbers which might be at risk. Close any fake accounts which have been opened in your name.

8. If any professional ID has been compromised get cards and passwords changed. If your passport, driving licence or National Insurance card has been stolen you must tell the relevant authorities. They will doubtless get back to you when they have had their tea and come back from holiday. To make sure that you can prove when you told them something write to them and post your letters by recorded delivery. Keep the recorded delivery slip as proof of your posting. Better still, get your lawyer to write to them.

9. Gather together all your own records and start a file dealing with the problem. (You should keep this for at least ten years after it's all over. If problems recur you will be glad you had it.)

10. Keep details of all the costs you incur. If you get a chance you may be able to sue the thief when you catch him.

11. Remember that you have a legal right to have incorrect information on your credit file corrected.

12. Go to your local police station to find out if any crimes have been committed in your name. Ask for details of any information held about you. (You are entitled to this under the Data Protection Act.)

83

Beware of companies, organisations and individuals offering 'identity theft protection' for a fee. Many of these people will tell you no more (and probably far less) than is in this book. I doubt whether anyone can protect you from identity theft better than you can. People who offer protection may claim that banks no longer provide protection for customers who are defrauded and that without insurance you may be liable for massive losses. Check with your bank that this is true before paying out premiums. And never, ever give out personal information to anyone offering to protect your identity.

84

Keep records of all your cards and bank accounts so that you can deal with identity theft as quickly as possible if your essential paperwork is stolen.

85

If your phone has a default PIN number (for example, protecting what used to be called your answering machine but is now, for reasons which no one can explain, known as your voice mail) then change it. Default PIN numbers for phones are widely known (and readily available over the Internet). If you leave the PIN number as it is other people can get into your voice mail. They can also change your message, redirect your phone calls and run up huge bills on your behalf.

86

If you possibly can, I suggest that you use a pay-as-you-go mobile telephone. If your phone is stolen (or a crook finds some other way to abuse your number) your liability should be limited to the amount of money you have put into your phone. If things get bad you can always destroy your phone and buy another.

87

Don't throw away (or give away) your mobile phone if you buy a replacement. If someone finds or buys your old phone and uses it for something illegal you could well find yourself answering questions from the police. At best this could be time consuming and embarrassing. At worse it could result in you spending thirty years in prison.

88

When you try to buy a mobile telephone from one of the big chains they will demand a vast amount of private information. Even if you buy with a credit card they still insist on having your full name and address. Some stores also insist on seeing other personal information. They treat everyone as a potential terrorist. Once, when I tried to make a purchase from a mobile phone shop and could only offer two credit cards as proof of my identity the assistant told me to go away and come back with a letter from my bank confirming that I was who I said I was. I duly went away. But you will not be surprised to hear that I did not go back.

These wretched people all say they want this information in order to protect the country from terrorists. Naturally, they usually manage to imply that if you refuse to answer their questions then you must either be a terrorist or a terrorist sympathiser.

But if you believe that you probably still sit around on Christmas Eve, waiting to catch a glimpse of Father Christmas sliding down your chimney.

I believe that the mobile phone companies want all that private information so that they can use it for commercial purposes and sell it to other companies. Don't feel obliged to give out more information than you feel they should have. If you are buying a pay-as-you-go telephone pay cash.

If you want to buy a mobile phone and don't want to give your name and address just visit a second-hand shop or car boot sale. Phones and SIM cards are easy to pick up. Because you don't know who else has used a second hand phone I would suggest that you put in a brand new SIM card before starting to use it. This will give you a new phone number and it will give the phone a new history.

Terrorists and criminals know this, of course, and so they are probably the only people in the world whose phones aren't tapped and whose calls are never listened to. The cleverer terrorists and criminals use each telephone just once. If you don't use a phone more than once your calls can never be traced.

The authorities haven't worked this out yet.

89

Be cautious when using your mobile telephone in a public place. Some phone users delight in speaking loudly enough for everyone around them to hear everything they say. Most of the time this is just rude and boring. But if they happen to be buying something by credit card over the phone then everyone within earshot will, at the end of the call, have all the information they need to use that person's card to buy themselves some goodies. Don't make that mistake.

90

Stay sceptical. I'm afraid that many people who get tricked out of their money deserve to be conned. Tricksters rely on people being so blinded by greed that their common sense goes out of the window. Are you really likely to win a lottery you have never even entered? Why should a complete stranger approach you and want to give you £2,000,000 to help him extricate £20,000,000 of his family's wealth which has got tied up in a complex confusion of bank accounts and is sitting, waiting to be collected, somewhere between Lagos and Amsterdam? The world is full of crooks. Many work for the Government. The worst wear smart suits and work for large, well-known companies. But all of them can ruin your life.

91

Keep a list of everything that is in your wallet, purse and handbag. I don't mean that you have to add up all the money every day. But do keep a list of the credit cards, bank cards, identity cards, keys and so on in each location. Also make a list of everything you keep in a home safe. Then add a list of the essential contact phone numbers you are likely to need. Put the whole package somewhere very safe (in a bank safe deposit box for example) so that you can get at it if you are mugged or burgled.

92

If you are using a credit card with a PIN number make sure that neither the sales assistant nor any other customers get to know what it is. (Sales assistants are more of a problem since they will also have access to your other card details). France has used credit cards with PIN numbers for as long as I can remember and their machines are all fitted with small guards so that when numbers are inputted it can be done confidentially. The British machines mostly seem to have been distributed without the guards (one shop assistant told me that they are still waiting for them). This probably saves the banks a couple of pence but it does expose you to a considerable risk. In the old days, when card transactions were confirmed with a signature it was the bank which took the main responsibility. Now that card transactions are confirmed with a PIN number the customer and the retailer take the responsibility. Having someone steal your PIN number by looking over your shoulder, or across the counter, could prove embarrassing, time consuming and very expensive.

93

If you think you may be a victim of an identity thief you can check your credit rating by contacting one of the following credit reference agencies which operate in Britain:

- Experian (www.experian.co.uk)
- Equifax (www.equifax.co.uk)

• Callcredit (www.callcredit.plc.uk)

You can use your local public library or the Internet to obtain up-to-date phone numbers and addresses.

94

Theoretically, it is illegal for anyone to open your mail. When you seal an envelope, put a stamp on it and pop it into the post box it is supposed to be sacrosanct until it reaches its destination and the person to whom it is addressed receives it and opens it. That's the theory. And it's a nice theory. In practice, however, life isn't quite so beautiful.

Leaving aside the growing number of postmen who seem to regard the sanctity of the mail as an anachronism (one postwoman in Plymouth was found to have over 100,000 letters and packets stored in her home) the fact is that the Government can and do open your mail whenever they feel like it.

There are no available figures for the UK (gosh, there's a surprise) but in the USA the authorities currently open around 500,000 packets a year. Just to see what they contain. They don't have warrants to do this. They just look, make a note of what the parcel contains and then send it on. Naturally, if they find that the recipient is buying items considered subversive there will no doubt be extra surveillance in the future.

The Government can look inside your mail in a number of ways. They can spray a solvent onto the envelope so that it becomes transparent and enables them to read what is inside. They can slip a knitting needle into the envelope roll the contents around the needle, read whatever you have written and then push the contents back into the envelope the same way they got them out. And, of course, they can use a kettle to steam open the envelope.

Actually, let's face it most of the time they could probably put your letter into an entirely fresh envelope when posting it on and you wouldn't be any the wiser. After all, you didn't see what the letter looked like when it was first put into the post box.

Finally, they can, of course, simply 'damage' your letter or packet so that they can take a look inside. I have one or two acquaintances whose mail always seems to get damaged – however carefully it is packed.

The authorities are particularly likely to peek at mail which is going abroad. For example, in the 1960s the American Internal Revenue Service routinely opened and photocopied all letters travelling between Switzerland and America – just in case any Americans were tucking away their savings in foreign bank accounts.

95

Here are some tips on protecting your mail:

1. Always assume that your mail is going to be read by people who shouldn't read it. The people most likely to tamper with your mail are those working for the Government and paid by you. (So you will be paying people to peek at your mail.)

2. Sending mail by recorded delivery or registered mail will not protect it from snoopers. Indeed, sending mail this way may actually draw attention to it – and, therefore, to you.

3. Many people put sticky tape on their envelopes to deter snoopers. I don't think this is a good idea. I suspect that if you do it then there may be an increased chance of your mail being opened or stolen. If you put sticky tape on an envelope to make it more secure you are drawing attention to your letter and making it clear that it contains something special.

4. Don't put your name and address on the back of an envelope. Just make sure the envelope is properly and clearly addressed. If you put your details on the envelope and the person to whom you have addressed your letter is on the Government's watch list then you will immediately be connected with them.

5. If you think your mail is being opened tell the postal authorities. Even if the Government is opening your mail your complaint will tell them that you know.

6. Ask friends just to put your address on your envelope. There

is no need for a name as well. Or use a false name.

7. If you suspect that your mail is being opened you can protect your outgoing mail by posting it from a different town and by varying the type of envelope you use. Print the envelope too if you have distinctive handwriting. Don't always use the same violet ink.

8. Consider using a courier service rather than the Post Office. This will make it slightly more difficult for the authorities to open your mail.

96

If you go away and have a glass front door your mail will be visible. It will be tempting to any confidence trickster who calls. Either ask a trusted neighbour to move your mail or arrange for the Post Office to hold your mail until you get back.

97

Make sure that you tell all those who matter your new address when you move. And pay the Post Office to forward your mail.

Each year around 200 million letters are delivered to an address where the recipient has 'gone away'. (And that's just the mail the Royal Mail knows about.) Much of that mail will contain confidential, valuable information.

98

If mail which you are expecting doesn't arrive, tell the sender. If you are sent credit card offers through the mail (these will often be completed with your name, address and other details) write to the banks concerned and demand that this is stopped. Tell them that if they don't stop doing it you will hold them responsible for any losses.

99

Take special care of your National Insurance number. Fraudsters can do quite a lot of damage if they have your name, address and National Insurance number.

100

Use a mail drop address or an accommodation address. These are now springing up all over the place. The advantage is that you can have your mail sent to an anonymous address and then mailed on to you. You can find details in the telephone directory under 'accommodation agencies' or look at the business services sections in *Exchange and Mart, Time Out, International Herald Tribune* or the *Economist*. If you can open an accommodation address without giving your real name then do so (but you will, of course, have to give an address at some time unless you are going to pick up your mail yourself.)

Alternatively, consider using a Post Office Box for your mail. Using a PO Box means that no one who doesn't need to have it, need ever know your exact address.

There are numerous advantages to using an accommodation address or a Post Office Box address.

For example, when you book a holiday and give your home address your travel agents get to know exactly when you are going away, where you are going and when you are coming back. In the bad old days the availability of this information would be limited to just a few people. But things are different now. Today, all your personal information will be fed into a computer. Hundreds, if not thousands, of people will have perfectly legal access to the information. If all of them are honest and uninterested in earning money by selling information to crooks you might come home and find your television set and stereo still where you left them.

Might.

Because now that all your details have been fed into a computer, any computer hacker who wants to know when you are going away, and how long you are going to be away, can find out quite easily.

Dismiss with a wave of a hand anyone who tells you that his

or her computer system is 'hacker proof'. There is no such thing. Hackers have even found their way into American military computers.

And so every time you book a holiday there is a very real chance of burglars having the time to break into your home and to remove every stick of furniture and even take your carpets. It happens.

In the dark old days before computers, the main danger was that you would forget to cancel the milk and the papers. But these days the burglars don't have to drive down your street looking for milk bottles lined up on your doorstep and newspapers sticking out of your letter box (actually, you're lucky if you still get milk and newspapers delivered these days).

Using a Post Office Box or mail drop address means that your travel agent doesn't know your home address. And it means that when you go away on holiday the crooks won't know which house to burgle.

101

I have been using a PO Box for personal mail for many years and have had no difficulty in arranging for gas bills, electricity bills, telephone bills, bank statements and other information to be sent there, although I have had some rather silly conversations.

'Your address is a PO Box?'

'Yes.'

'You live in a PO Box?'

'That's my address.'

'Isn't it a bit cramped?'

'They're quite roomy, really.'

'Oh.'

The only significant problem I've ever had was with a train company. I wanted to buy tickets over the telephone using a credit card which is registered to a PO Box address. 'I can only send tickets to the address to which your card is registered,' the railway employee said pompously. 'That's fine,' I replied. I gave him the PO Box address. 'Oh, we can't send tickets to a Post Office Box,' he said. 'For security reasons the company needs your full address before they will release any tickets.' He became quite belligerent when I pointed out that his argument was nonsensical. In the end I got bored with him. Instead of buying the cards by telephone, with a credit card, I walked to my local railway station and bought my tickets over the counter from the booking office clerk. I paid cash. The clerk didn't ask for my name or my address or even my inside leg measurement. The rail company's magnificently, pointlessly absurd security system wouldn't stop Bin Laden himself buying rail tickets if he took the trouble to turn up at the railway station.

102

If you are travelling you can have mail sent Post Restante at the local post office. Alternatively have it sent for you to collect at any hotel you intend to visit. Have the mail addressed to you as an 'arriving guest'.

103

If you need to send something private or valuable through the mail it is often quicker (and safer) to use the ordinary mail rather than 'recorded delivery' or 'registered delivery'.

To protect your correspondence from prying eyes (modern envelopes are often horribly thin) wrap your letter inside a page or two torn from a magazine. If you are sending bank notes through the post the same trick may help thwart any dishonest postman.

104

Don't accept any investment advice from the Government. When they aren't lying they are incompetent. When they aren't incompetent they are lying. If you kept your accounts the way the Government keeps its accounts you would be in prison. They lie. They cheat. They fiddle the figures. (They aren't even honest about inflation which is, any sensible observer knows, far higher than the Government says it is. As I explained in my book *Why Everything Is Going To Get Worse*, they brazenly fiddle the figures.)

105

Always assume that anything you say on the telephone is being overheard by your worst enemies. It probably is. Installing bugs on telephone lines isn't difficult. Even if the Government hasn't bugged your phone (and if you have ever been known to murmur dissent they probably already have) business rivals or commercial groups concerned about your activities can easily instal microphones to spy on you.

It is, of course, the Government which does the most phone tapping. In the old days (by which I mean before 1997 when Labour came into power) the police, MI5 and special branch would, between them, have had about 1,000 telephone taps in place. In most if not all of these cases they would have followed Home Office guidelines and had court permission for their taps. Today, the authorities no longer rely on 'official phone taps'.

Today, any line anywhere in the country can be routed through the Government's listening centres such as GCHQ in Cheltenham. Through such centres the Government can build up a dossier of the people you speak to and what you say to them. Evidence obtained by phone tap is banned in court in the UK because MI5 don't want to have what they do questioned or even discussed in court.

These days British agencies don't always bother to listen to phone conversations themselves. It is easier to get the Americans to do it.

There was a huge fuss in America in December 2005 when it became known that President Bush and his miserable men had been tapping the phones of Americans. But the Americans have been doing this to us for years. Indeed, the Americans have given themselves the authority to do anything they like anywhere in the world. The Americans use their national security agency which has listening stations all over the planet. They can listen in to landlines and satellite calls. There is for example a 500 acre

NSA listening station in Yorkshire. The place is largely staffed by Americans who, with the aid of dozens of satellite dishes and massive computers, monitor millions of phone and fax lines in the UK. They can listen to anything on any landline and can intercept all satellite communications, monitor fax lines, read e-mails and listen in to all mobile phone calls.

The Americans (and British Government agencies) listen in to some phone lines all the time. The rest of the time they use computers to trawl the system for key words and phrases. Once a key word is heard a tape recorder switches on and a human snoop listens in later. Naturally, no one knows what the key words are – though there are a lot of them. It's a good guess that words such as 'Blair', 'Bush', 'bomb', 'terrorism', 'war', 'explosive' and 'Iraq' are probably key words which will attract attention to your conversations.

You can't complain about any of this because officially it doesn't happen. And there are no British laws controlling what the Americans do in our country. There is no point in complaining to your MP if you think someone from the Government is listening in to your telephone conversations.

The Government claims that they need to listen to our telephone calls in order to find out what the terrorists are doing and in order to protect us from terrible things.

Having deliberately terrified us (and deliberately exposed us to the constant threat of terrorism) the Government claims that in order to protect us they need to take away our privacy and our liberty. Only by taking away our privacy and our liberty can they protect it. (This is like Casanova seducing a young girl and telling her that the only way for her to save her virginity is to surrender it to him.)

The Government make these absurd claims because they are crooks. I have described the reasons for these activities in greater length in other books – particularly in *Living in a Fascist Country.*

Journalists, broadcasters and commentators do and say nothing either because they are stupid and poorly informed or because they have been 'bought' with dinners in Downing Street and promises of MBEs and knighthoods in the honours list.

106

If you have stuck your head above the parapet then there is a greatly increased risk that your mail, telephone calls and e-mails will be scrutinised by the 'authorities'. Anyone who is politically active (I don't mean in a superficial, safe, ego and bank balance boosting pop star sort of way but in the genuine sense of putting yourself at risk in hope of making the world a better place) must assume that any telephone they use is tapped.

107

If you want to make a private phone call use a public phone box. I once got cut off during a radio interview. My home telephone mysteriously and inexplicably stopped working half way through an interview in which I was discussing something the Home Office had done. I ran to a nearby telephone box and completed the interview from there. When I got back home the telephone there was working again. It's difficult even for Government agencies to isolate, tap or cut off public phone boxes at a moment's notice. Naturally, you should not use the same public telephone box more than once. And you should be aware that CCTV cameras are often situated near to public phone boxes. However, this will not concern you since you will be merely trying to get a little privacy rather than doing anything dishonest or illegal.

108

Telephones are tapped all around the world these days. Thirty million Italians have had their phones tapped in the last ten years. They can't all be members of the Mafia.

109

Remember that mobile telephones emit a signal which tells the authorities where you are at any moment. If you want a little privacy, switch off the phone and let the answering machine catch your messages.

110

Don't be tempted to use telephone scramblers in order to have privacy. I believe it is illegal to use a scrambler which prevents the Government listening in to your calls. Even if you manage to find one which protects your conversations the authorities can force you to tell them the code being used. More importantly, using a scrambler suggests that you have something to hide and will attract attention to you.

111

Your phone companies (both for landline and mobile telephones) will keep a full record of all the calls you make. For mobile phone calls they will keep a record of where you were when you made the call. The companies will also keep a record of the calls you received. Companies are required by law to keep these records for a fixed time (which may be six months or a year) but you should assume that the call records will be kept indefinitely.

112

New digital telephone exchanges can connect your phone to a listening station even if your phone is on the hook. This turns your telephone into a microphone and enables the authorities to listen to everything you say.

113

Don't use a cordless phone unless you have no secrets. These telephones (which allow people to wander around inside the home and in the garden while using a landline) broadcast for up to two miles and anyone who wants to listen in can do so quite easily. This can be done accidentally as well as on purpose.

114

In Britain, you can find out who called you by dialling 1471. And you can block this facility by dialling 141 before the number you dial (or by having an automatic block put on all your outgoing calls). But if anyone really wants to find out who called they can do so by contacting the telephone company. And all your calls will appear on your telephone bill as usual.

115

If you don't want people to know where you live you can purchase an 0845 number from an organisation such as Phone Coop. Your callers will then not be able to identify the town where you live from the telephone code they dial. You can contact Phone Coop at www.thephone.coop

116

To avoid crank calls from people trying to sell you life insurance or double-glazing I suggest that you ask the phone company to give you an ex-directory number. This will mean that your number does not appear in the telephone book.

117

Remember that local authorities publish lists of everyone who lives in their area. And they sell these lists to just about anyone who wants to buy them. It is impossible to stop local authorities doing this – even though it is a clear breach of personal security. I know of individuals who fill in their local authority electoral roll form with a false name – and then say that the house they are living in is just a holiday home. They pay their full rates and so cannot be accused of doing anything fraudulent. This does keep their name off the electoral register. I should warn you that claiming that your home is a holiday home when it isn't will almost certainly be an offence since a failure to provide full and accurate information to a local authority can be punished with a fine. The penalty for providing misleading information will usually be printed on the council's forms. This approach is therefore, obviously not to be recommended.

118

Census forms only come round once a decade. The authorities always claim that they are treated confidentially. This is a lie. The information you put on a census form will be made available to all sorts of people. It may be sold to commercial companies. It may even be made available to your neighbours. A friend of mine who failed to complete his census form properly was shocked to find a particularly nosy neighbour standing on his doorstep one morning – clutching his census form. 'You haven't filled in this bit,' said the neighbour pointing to an empty box. It turned out that the nosy neighbour was working for the census authority which was apparently allowing its part-time employees to distribute and collect forms in their own neighbourhood. If you want to be private you should be very careful about what you put on a census form. You should, however, be aware that putting false information on a census form could result in you being fined.

119

Remember that telephone answering machines can be accessed fairly easily by people you don't know and that fax lines can be tapped. (You may be able to tease the fax tappers by faxing sideways.)

120

If you find that too many people have your telephone number, simply pay a fee and buy a new number. You can then start again – deciding who should have your new phone number.

121

If you have a fax machine the manual will tell you to put your name and telephone number into the machine's memory so that this information appears at the top of all the faxes you send. In some countries it is an offence not to make this information available. Sadly, I'm not very good with machines and have never managed to enter this information correctly.

122

If you ring an organisation which insists that you press a series of numbers before allowing you to do anything you may be able to bypass the system by keeping absolutely quiet. Eventually the robot voice will say something like 'I cannot identify the numbers you have given me and so I will now connect you with an agent'. You then get the enormous privilege of speaking to a live person. They might not be much use, but at least it will be someone to snarl at.

123

If you have a choice, avoid gold or platinum credit cards. When you hand over a gold card you are telling the shop assistant that you have money. (Actually, gold cards have been so debased that they don't really matter any more. But do avoid platinum cards and other cards which are marketed to those who want to tell the world that they are rich or super rich.)

124

Don't talk about your wealth and your bank accounts in public or to strangers. Being private is the best way to protect your privacy. Don't boast loudly to friends or relatives in pubs or restaurants. I have in the past sat quietly in a restaurant and learnt an enormous amount about the people at the next table (usually, far more than I wanted to know but often enough to cause them considerable harm should I have wanted to).

125

When travelling try to look like a simple tourist. Try to blend in wherever you are going. Try to be the grey man no one notices. If you attract attention you are likely to be the traveller who is selected to have his bags examined. The man in a three-piece pinstriped suit who comes off a holiday flight is just as likely to attract attention as the backpacker with long hair, greasy jeans and a dirty sweatshirt. And the traveller who stands out because he has expensive luggage, or is festooned with expensive cameras, is likely to attract the local crooks as soon as he wanders out of the airport.

126

If you have a choice between staying in a large hotel which belongs to a massive international chain or an equally good hotel which is locally owned choose the second. The hotel which is part of a chain will undoubtedly feed all your details into its computer and make them available to other companies worldwide.

127

Don't boast about your wealth or success in public. It is particularly important not to do this in local newspapers or on local TV. If the guy in the next street knows that you've just won a million pounds he may just trip over your gatepost and sue you for half of it (the million pounds not the gatepost).

128

Don't live in a flashy, ostentatious house which has burglar alarms plastered on the outside and CCTV cameras fixed all around. All this tells potential burglars that the house contains stuff which is worth protecting. (An ostentatious home is also likely to trigger a tax investigation.)

129

Don't pull a roll of notes out of your pocket when paying a bill with cash. Keep your money in smaller rolls. If you have a thick roll of notes you are making yourself an immediate target for pickpockets and muggers.

130

Try to pick your battles. Try hard to avoid unnecessary confrontations. Battle only when the battle is necessary and worth fighting. If you have constant small rows with the police, with your neighbours, with the local authorities and with every Government department you can think of you will be too exhausted to fight the important battles in life.

131

If you have enemies, or are in a legal dispute with someone, you should always assume that you are under surveillance of some kind. This is not paranoia, it is common sense. There are a growing number of spy shops where you can buy miniature video cameras, sophisticated microphones and other eavesdropping equipment. After the conclusion of one legal dispute in which I had been embroiled the opposition's solicitor sent me the file of paperwork his office had collected on me. They had far more newspaper cuttings on me than I had ever seen. They also had copies of private letters I had sent. I have no idea how they had obtained all this information.

132

Buy gold coins for security, but be aware that the Government may well choose to confiscate them in the future. Governments do this from time to time. Judging from what has happened in the past any compensation they pay you will be paltry. Gold bullion coins have the advantage that they don't rot and don't spoil. You can bury them in the garden, dig them up years later and they will be perfectly saleable. Don't try doing that with rare coins or with stamps or old books.

133

On the Internet you can obtain free software programmes that will enable you to take information from other people's computers and to monitor their every keystroke without them knowing. You don't want to do this. But other people may want to do this to you.

134

Some software sold over the Internet contains 'spyware' enabling the sellers to watch what you do on and with your computer.

135

The clothes you buy may contain invisible electronic tags which tell the seller everything he wants to know about you. The tags will enable watchers to 'follow' you and to see where you go. Since the shop from which you bought the `tagged' clothes will probably have your name and address they will soon know more about you than you know yourself.

136

You should try to keep a low profile and you should, wherever possible, avoid drawing attention to yourself. Yes, I know this sounds rather strange, coming from someone who writes and publishes books which draw attention to the shortcomings of the world's most powerful and vindictive terrorists. But this really is a case of 'do as I say, not what I do'.

The authorities (by which I mean the Government, the security services and the police) have for many years now kept extensive data bases on everyone who fails to toe the line. The authorities concentrate their inexhaustible energies and resources on keeping their files up-to-date.

137

If you write a letter complaining about some aspect of Government policy there is a good chance that you will end up on someone's black list. For example, if you send a letter of complaint to an organisation such as the BBC there is a chance that they may pass your name and address on to the 'authorities'. Your name may then be put in a 'black list' file and you may be honoured with visits from representatives of your local branch of the SS.

138

If you attend any sort of protest march you should expect to be filmed. For example, for as long as I can remember the police have been filming everyone who attends demonstrations and rallies protesting about vivisection. If the police are able to identify you from the film they have taken they may visit you at home or work even though you have broken no laws and done nothing wrong. If you go to a demonstration by car you should expect the police to write down your car number. (If you ask the police why they are doing this they will tell you they are doing it to help prevent car theft. Oddly enough, the police have only ever been seen writing down car numbers at demonstrations organised to protest about some aspect of Government policy.) At the end of the demonstration the police may follow you home. They may be able to find some reason to stop you and require you to present your 'papers' at a local police station. Alternatively, officers from a local police station may visit you at home or at work. Once again, you do not need to have done anything wrong to attract this sort of attention.

139

Don't hide things in bedside cabinets, dressing table drawers or the wardrobe. Those are the places where thieves look first. Don't hide things under the floorboards or in the attic if you expect them to remain undiscovered by professionals. Such hiding places will protect whatever it is you are trying to hide from 16-year-old opportunistic burglars looking for a TV set to steal but they won't provide much protection from serious thieves or searchers sent by some Government department. If you do have hiding places in your home make sure that they are really good ones. Otherwise, if searchers find one hiding place they will start looking for the others that they now suspect they may find. But remember that if you make your hiding place too difficult to access you will either not use it or you will become careless. When choosing hiding places be creative. Think of outhouses and garages for example.

140

Burglaries are increasing for two main reasons. First, the increase in drug use means that a rapidly expanding section of the population need to find huge amounts of money in order to satisfy their drug habit. Second, the failure of the police to take any interest in burglary (and the failure of the courts to punish burglars) mean that burglary has, for many, become the career of choice. It makes sense: overheads are low, there is no need to register for VAT and the chances of getting caught are incredibly low. If you do get caught the chances of being convicted are again incredibly low. And if you get caught and convicted the chances are good that your punishment will consist of a couple of free CDs and a surfing holiday somewhere sunny. Moreover, if a burglar has found the experience stressful or physically tiring he will be able to sue the householder for compensation.

There are, on the whole, two types of burglar.

There is the burglar who targets your home because you have the world's most expensive collection of jade stored in a glass fronted display case in the drawing room. He will know this because of the photographs of you and your home which he saw in 'Goodbye' magazine.

And there is the low-life sneak thief who needs money for his next fix or to pay his rates.

There is not much you can do about the first type of burglar (apart from keeping photographers out of your home).

But you may be able to trick the second type by using my 'mugger's wallet' philosophy in your home. Leave a box containing cheap costume jewellery on your dressing table or, better still, in your underwear drawer. Put the good stuff somewhere else. Leave a new (but cheap) wallet containing low denomination notes and a cheap watch on your bedside table.

141

If you want to visit a country and keep your travel arrangements private, fly first to a nearby country and then take a train.

142

If you have the option, choose to travel by rail rather than by aeroplane. Travelling by train is safer, less intrusive and more private. And you get to keep your nail scissors. Remember that flying is becoming increasingly hazardous – and it isn't just crashes which kill passengers. Recycled air on aeroplanes means that if one traveller on a plane has an infectious disease then it is quite likely that, by the end of the trip, every passenger will be infected too. China, New Zealand and Hong Kong have all declared that if a massive flu bug infection strikes they will quarantine visitors in aircraft hangars. This, I suspect, will pretty well guarantee that everyone in the hangar will catch whatever bugs everyone else is carrying.

143

It's a nuisance, but you should always use different passwords for different accounts. If you use the same password and a crook gets hold of it he will be able to rifle through all your accounts in no time at all.

144

Different banks make different security demands. If you go to one bank which makes unreasonable demands on you, go somewhere else.

145

If you find yourself in trouble in a foreign country it is safest to assume that your government will not lift a finger to help you. The Government will have its own agenda, and embassy employees will have their own priorities. Their loyalties will not be to you. It is unwise to rely on politicians or diplomats for help.

The best way to get out of trouble is to use the media. Contact the news desk of a national newspaper (preferably a tabloid newspaper) and explain your plight.

Politicians and diplomats will, of course, warn you that contacting the media could endanger your position. Translated, this means that if you contact the media you will embarrass them.

The media will not help you out of compassion. They will only help you if you have a good story to tell them. So make your story a good one. Feed them something to excite them.

146

The size and significance of the Internet is often exaggerated (both by its fans and its enemies). According to OECD data, published in October 2005, the Internet is nowhere as ubiquitous as some Internet companies would have you believe. The OECD survey showed that only 66.3% of large and medium sized British companies have their own website. In other countries the figures are even more striking. In Spain, only 39.7% of large and medium sized companies have a website. In Portugal the figure is 29.4%. And in France just 26.3% of large and medium sized companies have their own website. Three quarters of France's most important companies still don't think that the World Wide Web is significant enough for them to have a website. Whatever its proponents may claim for it, there seems little doubt that the Internet is, today, little more than a massive car boot sale and porn shop.

I suggest that you use the Internet in just three ways:

First, for research (with great scepticism, unless you know and trust the website you are consulting). Search engines have corrupted the whole principle of research by selling positions on their results lists. So, if you do a search on a vitamin, for example, you may find that the top results will all be for sites selling vitamins and, therefore, having a vested interest in promoting the value of the vitamin. Contrary to the popular impression the Internet has made fair and proper research more, not less, difficult since some sites masquerading as independent sites are sponsored or paid for by commercial organisations.

Second, as a shopping mall (preferably buying items from people whom you are happy to trust).

Third, as a communications medium. But if you use e-mail do so with great caution and an awareness that nothing on the Internet is private.

I don't think the Internet is suitable (i.e. safe enough) for banking, making investments or paying bills. Your bank will offer all sorts of inducements to persuade you to do so. They will offer you a higher rate of interest on your deposit account. They will promise you cheaper dealing for your brokerage account. Their costs will be much lower for online banking. But, if you care about your privacy, you should resist the bank's inducements.

The biggest danger to your personal and financial security does not come from outside hackers but from the bank itself.

And I certainly wouldn't fill in my tax form online.

If you don't have and don't want Internet access (or you have it but want to be cautious about how you use it) don't be embarrassed to refuse to pay your bills online. Don't feel pressurised by large companies who push you to do things online. Always remember that their enthusiasm for the Internet is inspired by the fact that things are cheaper for them if you use the Internet.

147

If you run a business on the Internet, do be careful not to put all your eggs in one basket. Remember that the Internet is controlled by the Americans whose whims are unpredictable and who treat the rest of the world as second-class. Remember too that it is by no means inconceivable (indeed, it is regarded as pretty much a certainty by security experts in the industry) that the entire Internet will at some stage be shut down by terrorists. How many companies which now operate solely on the Internet would survive a shutdown that lasted for several months?

148

To protect yourself against computer fraud make sure that your security system is up-to-date. Many viruses rely on the fact that your computer has not been updated or protected for some time. Don't download or accept files or attachments from people you don't know or don't do business with. Downloading pirated 'free' software is a sure way to get infected. Most home computers in Britain are already infected with software which transmits information to other computers. Beware of opening e-mail attachments, even from friends. This is the way most viruses spread. If possible, use two computers: one for work and private, confidential material and one for the Internet. This is particularly important if you do creative work of any kind. When you protect yourself online with a password make sure that you choose a good one. Most people use ordinary dates and the names of children or pets as passwords. These are rarely difficult to guess. They are always easy to break if the thief uses an automated word checker to try out word after word until they find the right one. Use passwords which contain a mixture of letters and numbers. Or combine several words to create a new word that cannot be found with a computer programme. Never use the same password more than once.

149

When filling in computer forms which ask for personal information I strongly suggest that you resist the temptation to tell the truth whenever it is legally and morally proper for you to do so. When opening an e-mail account, for example, you would have to be barking mad to give all the information which is so often demanded. Why should these anonymous people know your mother's maiden name or your favourite colour, hometown or best friend? This is all vital information which an identity thief may be able to use. I think I'm safer making up stuff and keeping a note of stuff I may need to re-submit than I am giving out accurate personal information.

150

Be careful to destroy pre-printed mailshots from banks and other institutions offering you credit cards and loans. These mailshots often have your name, address and other personal details already printed on them. If you throw away one of these mailshots a thief who takes it from your dustbin can easily open an account in your name. (Yet again, here is proof that banks don't really give a damn about protecting the country from terrorists and criminals.) These pre-printed application forms, distributed by the million, are one of the easiest ways criminals can use to steal your identity and your money.

151

There is no computer system anywhere in the world which is completely safe from crooks. It is safest to assume that anything which is put into a computer will, sooner or later, be stolen. Distrust anyone who boasts that his or her computer system cannot be broken into. Their naivety endangers your security.

152

When your computer says 'Remember this password?' say 'No!' very firmly. Don't allow your computer to save your passwords for you. This is a bad, lazy habit to get into. It means that when you leave your desk your computer will be 'open' to anyone who passes by.

153

If you are trying to protect something on the Internet, then I suggest you change your password regularly. Once every three months should be fine.

154

When you are shopping on the Internet I believe that credit cards provide slightly better protection than debit cards.

155

When e-mail was first introduced, computer geeks sneered at people who still wrote letters and put them into the post. Such correspondence was known, rather derisively, as 'snail mail'. The same computer geeks dismissed fax machines as archaic, relics of another age.

Today, a growing number of people have realised that sending messages by e-mail is about as private as using an aerosol spray can to write on walls.

E-mail is fine for 'fun' correspondence.

But you should never, ever use it for anything that you would like to keep even a teeny bit confidential.

156

Posted letters and messages sent by fax might be old-fashioned but they definitely offer the best protection from snoopers. In September 2005 a study by an anti-spyware company found that the UK has one of the highest rates of spyware infection in the world, with an average of 18 spy programmes on every computer. Only the USA and Thailand have higher rates.

(Spyware is software that monitors computer users' activities – often without their knowledge. Companies may, for example, plant software on users' computers in order to deliver pop-up advertisements or to collect marketing data about them. This sort of software can slow computer performance by up to 90%. These malicious programmes are estimated to cost £445 million a year in lost time, productivity and computer repairs.)

157

Even banks are now becoming aware of the dangers of e-mail. For example, I recently saw this:

'Please do not transmit orders or instructions regarding a UBS account by e-mail. The information provided in this e-mail or any attachments is not an official transaction, confirmation or account statement. For your protection, do not include account numbers, Social Security numbers, credit card numbers,

passwords or other non-public information in your e-mails.'
UBS is one of the world's largest banks.

158

The hazards of using e-mail are made worse by the fact that the large American corporations which dominate the Internet seem to put commercial expediency above the rights of their customers and have been accused of not just turning a blind eye to the abuses of the Chinese Government (as both the American and British Governments routinely do) but actually collaborating with them. For example:

♦ Google, the Internet search engine has been criticised for tailoring the results of its Chinese search service to exclude websites which are blocked by the Chinese Government.

♦ MSN, the online branch of Microsoft, has been accused of being too willing to help the Chinese Government control the Internet. For example, MSN has banned the words 'freedom' and 'democracy' from parts of its search engine in China on the grounds that these words are 'forbidden'.

♦ Yahoo has been accused by Reporters Without Borders (a Paris based press freedom watchdog) of providing the Chinese Government with information which enabled it to convict a journalist who had revealed information about the Communist Party's propaganda department's plans for the anniversary of the Tiananmen Square demonstration. With the help provided by Yahoo! the journalist was jailed for ten years. Yahoo! says that its decision is the cost of doing business in China.

159

Many users are unaware of just how sophisticated computer systems have become.

Adobe Systems, the firm behind the popular portable-document-format (PDF) files that are widely e-mailed, has found a way to turn paper into computer code. Adobe is now putting a barcode at the bottom of its latest PDF documents. As a PDF form is filled in on the computer so the barcode constantly changes so that information is captured. The barcode records the obvious information (the user's name and address etc) but also details of who else has read the form, who may see it and who needs to see it. When the form is printed and sent on as a piece of paper the recipient only needs to scan the paper in order for the information to be sucked off the barcode.

The significance of this is that when you fill in a form online and print it out you may (not unreasonably) assume that the form contains only the information you can see.

Not true.

160

Don't lend your computer to anyone. If they use your computer to access an illegal site (e.g. a site offering paedophile pictures) you will be the one the police will arrest. Do you really want to try talking your way out of that?

161

Be very, very careful if anyone wants to put your signature onto a computer screen (usually via a small hand-held device). They will tell you that they want to store your signature 'so that we can help protect your security'). Resist this nonsense with all your strength. Once your signature is sitting neatly in a computer anyone will be able to use it. This is an appalling breach of security since once your signature is in the system it can be used or copied by anyone with dishonest motives. I am appalled at how many companies now invite customers to sign hand-held computers.

162

When your computer breaks down (as it will do one day) I suggest that you undo all the screws you can find and throw away your computer in pieces. Destroy the hard drive. Repairing a computer which has broken will probably cost more than buying a new one (or a new second-hand one). Repairs take time and are troublesome. Any computer or printer more than twelve months old will be looked upon as an antique. You will probably be able to buy something much more powerful for very little extra.

Why not simply give your computer away to someone? Two reasons.

First, before you can do this you will have to format and reformat your hard drive to try and remove everything left on it. Even then you will probably be giving away a computer which contains personal and private material. If the recipient really wants to, he will probably be able to see what you've been doing. You may not mind that.

But, second, in these strange days there is always the danger that the person who acquires your computer may do things with it which are illegal. Then, when he is arrested for having pictures of small children on his computer, or for planning some terrible crime, he will claim that this material isn't his but must have been the work of the previous owner.

Clank.

That's the sound of the cell door banging behind you.

163

Computers are good for storing private information. But remember that if the bad guys get into your house they can easily suck everything off your computer. They may even be able to do it from outside your house if you use a wireless system to connect your computer to the Internet.

164

Reformat old disks which contain information you don't need but which you want to use again. Just erasing files doesn't get rid of them. If the disks are old then destroy them. Break the disk apart, tear out the floppy disk and cut it up into tiny pieces with scissors.

165

Assume that you cannot remove information from a computer hard drive. If you have a hard drive which you want to clear I suggest that you beat it with a hammer until it is bent in two, put it on a fire for a couple of hours and then bury it deep in the ground somewhere.

166

Write delicate personal correspondence in RAM only. Don't store such letters except as pieces of paper.

167

Encryption is a waste of time. It gives a false sense of security and attracts attention from the very people you may be trying to avoid. Since the Government can force you to give them codes and passwords encryption is pointless.

168

Don't use online data stores. It may sound attractive to be able to store your private files in cyberspace but you would have to be a lunatic to do any such thing.

169

Always assume that the whole world can read anything you write in an e-mail. The most convenient e-mail addresses are the ones which are obtainable from websites such as hotmail and hushmail. I don't believe these are any more secure than any other e-mail addresses but at least you can access your mail when you are travelling. When you delete unwanted e-mails they go into a 'deleted folder'. To get rid of them you must delete them from there too. But even then they will still be on your hard drive. Don't believe any computer expert who tells you that he can remove e-mails from your computer by reformatting or fragmentation.

170

Never respond to spam e-mail. Even sending a letter of complaint is a mistake. You will merely establish that your e-mail address is operative and you will end up getting still more e-mail.

171

Turn on the 'cookies' warning on your browser. Then when a website wants to put a cookie on your hard-drive you can decide whether or not to accept it. Cookies are bits of data stored on your computer's hard drive. They contain your passwords to various sites and can be used to keep track of the websites you visit. Among other things.

172

Remember that your computer keeps track of all the websites you visit. For ever.

173

Be wary of how much information about yourself you give to people whom you meet online. Many web users routinely lie about their age, sex and appearance. When visiting sites which demand personal information be wary about how much information you give. And be wary about what you withhold. In some countries you may have a legal liability to tell the truth when using the Internet. Remember that Britons can now be (very easily) extradited from a good many countries in the world (including the USA and the whole of the EU). If you break a law in a foreign country you may find yourself being taken there to stand trial. This has happened. It can happen to you.

174

Bad people can instal something called a Magic Lantern on your computer. A Magic Lantern will record every keystroke you make and then transmit the information to the installer. This can happen without you being aware of it.

175

Trojan horses, which you can pick up from e-mails you receive and from websites you visit, can make a list of your passwords, transmit all your private files to another computer, log all your keystrokes and control your computer.

176

Remember that free software, picked up on the web, may contain all sorts of viruses and spies which watch over what you do with your computer.

The viruses can be used to spy on your computer (to see what you do and say), to listen to your conversation and to obtain your bank details.

177

Hackers have now created computer viruses which allow them to download child porn (or anything else) onto your computer without you knowing. The virus allows the hacker to download his child porn and store the images on your computer without you having the faintest idea what has happened. The paedophile/hacker can, of course, upload his stored images whenever he wants. Naturally, if the police investigate you will be the one trying to explain that you didn't download the material and that you didn't know it was there. Good luck.

178

As a computer user you should always assume that the bad guys are much better at peeping than you are at drawing the curtains.

179

As many bankers and investment analysts have discovered (to their embarrassment and financial cost) e-mails are for ever. Once you send an e-mail it cannot be erased. You may, of course, be able to remove it from your own computer by destroying the hard drive but you will not be able to remove it from the recipient's computer and the parts of the Internet which were used to transmit the message. Whenever you write an e-mail you must assume that it will, in the future, be available to a wide audience.

180

Electronic communications are now widely regarded as crucial evidence by the courts. A failure to produce e-mails can lead to disastrous consequences. For example, in the USA a Florida State judge instructed a jury to assume that Morgan Stanley was at fault because the bank could not produce electronic documents which the judge had demanded. The damages for failing to produce the required e-mails were $850 million.

181

If you want to invest money but don't have the requisite number of gas bills it is worth remembering that the Government's National Savings people will happily take your money without seeing your gas bills or demanding your passport. All they want is a cheque and your name and address. They do warn that they 'may search data at a credit reference agency' though I suspect that they don't always do this. They only require documentary evidence of identity and address from people who live outside the UK. You can buy national savings certificates, bonds, gilts and premium bonds this way. (So, if a Government agency is content to trust its customers just why do banks require so much information?)

182

If you are a celebrity (and these days a growing number of 'ordinary' people are, through so-called reality programmes, becoming famous) you should be careful about how much information you give to journalists. A huge number of celebrities were defrauded of millions by a trainee dishwasher using the Internet and a copy of a magazine's 'Richest People In America' list. Many celebrities regularly tell television audiences where and when they are going on holiday, apparently unaware that their home addresses are easy to identify.

183

Having been brought up in a fairly free society most of us have got used to not having to defend our privacy or our identity. We talk openly about private things. We discuss financial or employment issues at work and in restaurants. We regard conversations on the telephone as confidential. We don't have anything to hide and so we don't bother to hide anything.

Sadly, this attitude is now as out-of-date and as dangerous as leaving your front door open when you pop to the shops. We live in an increasingly dangerous world. And it is becomingly increasingly hazardous to expose your private world to outside scrutiny.

Don't tell outsiders things unless they need to know. Don't talk about personal issues to strangers. Don't talk openly about your holiday or travel plans. (An increasing number of thieves burgle houses which they know will be empty because they have received information from someone working in a travel agency or a holiday company.) If you are travelling don't write your home address on your luggage. (Otherwise everyone who handles – or even sees – your luggage will know that you are going away.)

It is often tempting to share things with other people. But beware. Even if you tell someone something in secret the chances are high that it will be spread to others. And every time a piece of information is passed along it becomes increasingly distorted and less and less private. Finally, remember that the greatest threats to your security, your identity and your privacy come from people whom you used to feel able to trust: people such as policemen, doctors and bank managers. Don't tell bank staff more than they really must know. Don't be afraid to refuse to give information. Don't give your doctor more information than he needs to treat you. And don't give a policeman any information he isn't legally entitled to demand.

184

Identity cards, when they are introduced, will make your identity easier to steal. (There is a lengthy explanation for this assertion in my book *Living In A Fascist Country*.)

185

Here is some advice that will help you avoid having your identity stolen:

1. Check that your bank statements, telephone bills and utility statements arrive on time. If they don't then there is a chance that they have been stolen and could be misused.

2. Obtain copies of your credit report once every three months. This shouldn't cost more than a few pounds. Check for anything that seems suspicious.

3. Never, ever discard personal papers (i.e. anything which contains your name and or your address) in the dustbin.

4. Don't leave cheque books, bank statements etc lying around at home. Put them somewhere as safe as you can.

5. If you are asked to fill in forms, make sure you know what you are filling in, and that the institution is entitled to ask for the information it wants.

6. If asked to give your secret password or identification number over the telephone never, ever give the whole password. Ask the bank employee (or whoever) to ask you specific letters or numbers from the word or code (e.g. ask them to ask you the 2nd, 4th and 6th letters or numerals).

7. Don't give out any personal information unless you have to.

If someone claims to represent a government department or a bank make sure that you refuse to hand over information until you know whom you are talking to.

8. Much ID theft is done by visitors to your home. Watch out for employees and callers. Don't leave cheque books, statements etc lying around.

9. Don't carry all your credit cards in one wallet. (And have as few as possible). Report stolen cards immediately. Change PIN numbers regularly. Beware of cameras and loiterers when you are getting money out of a cash machine.

186

Some married women like to keep their maiden name for work. This can confuse banks and other institutions. On balance this is probably a good thing. If you confuse the banks you will probably also confuse the identity thieves.

187

Be particularly wary when dealing with American companies. There are few laws to protect customer privacy in the USA and most companies will sell your details to anyone. European laws require Internet users to 'opt in' to allow merchants to sell their private details. In most areas of America an 'opt out' clause is allowed. In other words, unless you explicitly request otherwise, whatever data you have given the company will be resold to anyone who wants to buy it. The American system is designed to protect companies and profits and not to protect individuals and their privacy. One American data mining company happily sold the work address of a woman who was being stalked. They sold her address to the man who was stalking her. He murdered her as she left her office. You should be aware, too, that the American Government gets round the protection provided to individuals by the American Constitution by purchasing data from data collection companies. The Federal Bureau of Investigation routinely uses the services of data collection companies.

188

Make sure your family and friends read this book and understand just how vulnerable we all are. There is little point in you taking precautions to protect your identity, security and privacy if other members of your family are careless or unaware.

The Author

Instinctively anti-authority and recklessly uncompromising, Vernon Coleman is the iconoclastic author of over 90 books which have sold over 2 million copies in the UK, been translated into 23 languages and now sell in over 50 countries. His best-selling non-fiction book *Bodypower* was voted one of the 100 most popular books of the 1980s/90s and was turned into two television series in the UK. The film of his novel *Mrs Caldicot's Cabbage War* was released early in 2003. In the 1980s, although several of his books had been high in the best-seller lists, he got fed-up with nervous publishers trying to edit all the good bits out of his books and so he started his own publishing conglomerate which began life in a barn and now employs five people.

Vernon Coleman has written columns for the *Daily Star, The Sun, Sunday Express, Planet on Sunday* and *The People* (resigning from the latter when the editor refused to publish a column questioning the morality and legality of invading Iraq) and has contributed over 5,000 articles, columns and reviews to 100 leading British publications including *The Daily Telegraph, Sunday Telegraph, The Guardian, The Observer, The Sunday Times, Daily Mail, Mail on Sunday, Daily Express, Woman, Woman's Own, Punch* and *Spectator*. His columns and articles have also appeared in hundreds of leading magazines and newspapers throughout the rest of the world. He edited the *British Clinical Journal* for one year until a drug company told the publisher to choose between firing him or getting no more advertising. For twenty years he wrote a column which was syndicated to over 40 leading regional newspapers. Eventually, the column had to be abandoned when Government hired doctors offered to write alternative columns without charge to stop him telling readers the truth. In the UK he was the TV AM doctor on breakfast TV and when he commented that fatty food had killed more people than Hitler he wasn't fired until several weeks after a large food lobbyist had threatened to pull all its advertising. He was the first networked television Agony Aunt. In the past he has presented TV and radio programmes for both BBC and commercial channels though these days no producer who wants to keep his job for long is likely to invite him anywhere near a studio (especially a BBC studio). Many millions consulted his Telephone Doctor advice lines and have visited his websites, and for six years he wrote a monthly newsletter which had subscribers in 17 countries. Vernon Coleman has a medical degree, and an honorary science doctorate. He has worked for the Open University in the UK and is an honorary Professor of Holistic Medical Sciences at the Open International University based in Sri Lanka. He used to give occasional lectures but these days the invitations are usually withdrawn when big companies find out about it.

Vernon Coleman has received lots of really interesting awards from people he likes and respects. He is, for example, a Knight Commander of The Ecumenical Royal Medical Humanitarian Order of Saint John of Jerusalem, of the Knights of Malta and a member of the Ancient Royal Order of Physicians dedicated to His Majesty King Buddhadasa. In 2000 he was awarded the Yellow Emperor's Certificate of Excellence as Physician of the Millennium by the Medical Alternativa Institute. He is also Vice Chancellor of the Open International University. He has not been offered, and would not accept, any award by the British Government.

He worked as a GP for ten years (resigning from the NHS after being fined for refusing to divulge confidential information about his patients to State bureaucrats) and has organised numerous campaigns both for people and for animals.

He collects hobbies and accumulates books. He is a long-term member of the MCC. He has been intending to learn to speak French for over half a century but has made very little progress. He can ride a bicycle and swim, though not at the same time. He loves cats, cricket (before they started painting slogans on the grass), cycling, cafes and, most of all, the Welsh Princess.

Vernon Coleman is balding rapidly and is widely disliked by members of the Establishment. He doesn't give a toss about either of these facts. Many attempts have been made to ban his books but he insists he will keep writing them even if he has to write them out in longhand and sell on street corners (though he hopes it doesn't come to this because he still has a doctor's handwriting). He is married to Donna Antoinette, the totally adorable Welsh Princess, and is very pleased about this. Together they have written two books *How To Conquer Health Problems Between Ages 50 And 120* and *Health Secrets Doctors Share With Their Families.*

Publishing House

Publishing House (and its imprints: Chilton Designs, the European Medical Journal and Blue Books) doesn't have a massive sales force (actually, it doesn't have a sales force at all). Publishing House doesn't have a board of eminent directors (since it's not a limited company it doesn't have any directors). Publishing House doesn't have offices in a skyscraper (it does have offices but just an upstairs and a downstairs). And there is no PR department full of bright young things called Hyacinth and Jacaranda. (There isn't a PR department at all).

But Publishing House has one enormous advantage over the conglomerates.

Publishing House cares passionately about books.

The big multinational publishers have marketing departments which decide which books will sell. They then commission books that the sales force think they will be able to flog. They won't even consider a book until they've done a marketing feasibility study.

Publishing House publishes books it thinks should be published and then tries to sell them. Naturally, Publishing House tries to make a profit. If it didn't it wouldn't last long. There are printing bills, electricity bills, phone bills, rates, insurance and so on to be paid. And there are no outside sponsors or advertisers and no benevolent backers.

Publishing House has been in business since 1988. Its books

have been translated into 22 languages and are sold by other publishers (including some big ones) in over 50 countries. Large print and audio versions of some books are available. One has been made into a film.

The big publishers insist that every book should make a profit.

Publishing House doesn't work like that. Some books make more money than others. But that's fine. As long as the better sellers subsidise the other books. Publishing House doesn't mind if a book is a little slow to sell. Like good parents, Publishing House loves all its children equally – however successful, or unsuccessful, they might be.

Despite all the talk about the need for each book to stand on its own two feet many big publishers make an overall loss. They are kept alive – effectively as vanity publishers – by other parts of the conglomerate. So, for example, the TV division or the magazine division may help to subsidise the book publishing division.

Publishing House believes that book publishing can, and should, be allowed to stand alone. Moreover, Publishing House believes that small publishers are now the only *real* publishers in existence.

Big publishers often accept sponsorship from outside companies. Publishing House never does, but prefers to rely on the sale of books to pay the bills. No Publishing House books are sponsored or carry any advertising. There is no outside advertising or sponsoring on the website. It is this which enables us to remain truly independent. Publishing House publishes books which international conglomerates wouldn't dare touch.

Big publishers are too market orientated and derivative. They produce more of what other publishers did well with last year. Publishing House looks forwards not backwards.

Big publishers pay huge amounts as advances to film stars, politicians and young hot shot authors. Much of the time they don't earn back those advances. They don't care because the books are just seen as 'tools' to help other parts of the empire. For example, a conglomerate will publish a politician's dull biography as a way of putting money into the politician's pocket.

Big publishers worry enormously about upsetting powerful

politicians and other corporations. The big conglomerates need to cooperate with the establishment because they are part of the establishment.

Publishing House stands outside the establishment and doesn't give a fig for what politicians or corporate bosses might (or might not) think. Publishing House is only interested in publishing books that inform and entertain. And Publishing House fights for its books and for their survival.

At big publishers there are loads of men and women in suits who slow things down and interfere with the artistic process. Literary originality and integrity have been replaced by marketing convenience. Publishing House has no men or women in suits to decide on policy. Publishing House does what seems right.

Publishing House publishes books the old-fashioned way. Because there are no worries about upsetting establishment figures it can publish books that large, modern commercial publishers would never dare publish.

Publishing House is a small, independent publishing house which publishes books it believes in and which it hopes that its readers will want to read.

Also by Vernon Coleman

Living in a Fascist Country

Conspiracies, peak oil, greedy politicians, endless religious wars and your disappearing freedom and privacy

"We are losing our freedom and our privacy. Everything we hold dear is being threatened by the New Order. The world is changing so fast that it is difficult to keep up. Britain and America are now fascist states. Why? What is going on? Whatever happened to democracy? Who is behind it all? How did we come to find ourselves in what the politicians boast will be an everlasting war?

You will, I hope, find at least some of the answers in this book. The way the Government is clamping down on free speech this may well be your last chance to read the truth."

Vernon Coleman

Paperback £15.99
Published by Blue Books
Order from Publishing House • Trinity Place • Barnstaple •
Devon EX32 9HG • England
Telephone 01271 328892 • Fax 01271 328768
www.vernoncoleman.com

Also by Vernon Coleman

Why Everything Is Going To Get Worse Before It Gets Better

(And What You Can Do About It)

Why Everything Is Going To Get Worse Before It Gets Better explains why things are so bad, why things are going to get worse, how we can rescue ourselves, how we can save our country and what we can do to protect ourselves and our loved ones in the meantime.

Vernon Coleman explains why our health service is so bad that asylum seekers go home for treatment when they fall ill, why our education system is so bad that illiteracy is now commonplace, why millions no longer respect the courts or the police and why virtually no one now trusts our financial institutions. He explains how we've been betrayed by our Government (which has taken away our freedom and our privacy and which deliberately uses fear to promote its policies), why our lives are run not by people but by organisations and why we are now living in a fascist State – where the rights of individuals come second to the demands of the system.

Why Everything Is Going To Get Worse Before It Gets Better is both terrifying and yet, in the end, reassuring. Vernon Coleman shines light into dark corners, explains precisely what has gone wrong (and why) and offers original solutions.

Because he believes that things will get worse before they get better he also offers practical advice designed to help readers survive the painful years ahead.

Paperback £15.99
Published by Blue Books
Order from Publishing House • Trinity Place • Barnstaple •
Devon EX32 9HG • England
Telephone 01271 328892 • Fax 01271 328768
www.vernoncoleman.com

Also by Vernon Coleman

England Our England
Sound reasons to reject the euro and the EU

'The European Union is widely regarded as a rather annoying joke. When people think of the EU they think of butter mountains, wine lakes and daft rules about straight bananas.

There is a nationwide tendency to think that the crooked, laughably incompetent officials in Brussels are somehow irrelevant and insignificant to our daily lives; no more than an expensive, international extension of the civil service.

But the EU is no joke.

There has been squabbling and fighting in Europe for three millennia. Caesar, Charlemagne, Pope Innocent III, Napoleon and Hitler all tried to unite these countries under a single flag. They all failed.

It is no exaggeration to say that the European Union poses the greatest threat to democracy, and to our freedom and privacy, that there has ever been. .

In an attempt to explain the truth – and to warn you of what is happening to your world – I've prepared a summary of some of the things you should know about the European Union; facts which the main political parties certainly won't tell you. Your TV station, radio station and newspaper probably haven't warned you about these things.

As you read this book remember that this is not a piece of science fiction. These are not bizarre, paranoid fantasies.

This may turn out to be the most frightening book you've ever read. But everything in it is true.'

Vernon Coleman

Paperback £8.99
Published by Blue Books
Order from Publishing House • Trinity Place • Barnstaple •
Devon EX32 9HG • England
Telephone 01271 328892 • Fax 01271 328768
www.vernoncoleman.com

Also by Vernon Coleman

Saving England
The Case for Independence

"This book is about England rather than Britain for an excellent reason. If the EU's plans for Britain are carried through to completion it will only be England which will disappear. Scotland and Wales will retain their identity as regions of the new European superstate. England, however, will disappear and will be converted into nine anonymous regions.

Whereas it is widely perceived as a 'good thing' when Scottish and Welsh nationalists fight for the identity and independence of their nations, England nationalists are neither thick on the ground nor well respected.

If we don't do anything to save her, England is doomed. It will be no good saying 'We should have done something' when our nation has become a footnote in the history books. It is up to us to do something. And we must act soon. The main part of this book explains just why we must act. The final part of this book explains what we must do."

From the Foreword to *Saving England* by Vernon Coleman

Paperback £8.99
Published by Blue Books
Order from Publishing House • Trinity Place • Barnstaple •
Devon EX32 9HG • England
Telephone 01271 328892 • Fax 01271 328768
www.vernoncoleman.com

Also by Vernon Coleman

Rogue Nation

How and why the USA threatens your home, family, health, freedom and future.

"America has the biggest stocks of weapons of mass destruction – and is the nation least likely to use those weapons responsibly.

America is now the world's most dangerous enemy. America is a rogue nation, bullying its way into authority and power; unsettling other countries and constantly starting wars. America is responsible for worldwide economic and political chaos.

Most Americans think they are fighting terrorists. Most of the rest of the world knows that Americans now are the terrorists.

This book contains everything you need to know – and must know – about America."

Vernon Coleman

"*Rogue Nation* is a great read. I've read Michael Moore's books but yours does edge the others in terms of not apologising at all or shilly-shallying around the subject" P.E., BATH

"Your best yet. Congratulations on all the research." E. P., FRANCE

"*Rogue Nation* should be compulsory reading ..." C. B., BY E-MAIL

"Having read some of your other works where you exposed some of the sophistry cant and humbug with which the medical profession is replete I wondered how you would deal with this subject. I was not disappointed." W. M., London

"I am very impressed with *Rogue Nation*. When I started to read it, I just could not put it down. A truly explosive book with a mine of information." T. C., Sussex

Paperback £9.99
Published by Blue Books
Order from Publishing House • Trinity Place • Barnstaple •
Devon EX32 9HG • England
Telephone 01271 328892 • Fax 01271 328768
www.vernoncoleman.com

Also by Vernon Coleman

Spiritpower

Discover your spiritual strength

- Find out who you are (and what you want)
- Three words that can change your life
- How to get what you want out of life
- Use your imagination and your subconscious mind
- Why you have more power than you think you have
- How you can control your own health
- Why you shouldn't be afraid to be a rebel
- How to stand up for yourself
- Know your fears and learn how to conquer them

What the papers say about *Spiritpower*:

'*The final tome in his trilogy which has produced the best-sellers "Bodypower" and "Mindpower", this is Dr Coleman's assessment of our current spiritual environment, and his prescriptions for change. He advises both awareness and rebellion, recommending ways to regain personal autonomy and fulfilment.*'
(The Good Book Guide)

'*"Spiritpower" will show you how to find freedom and give meaning to your life.*'
(Scunthorpe Evening Telegraph)

'*This is a handbook for tomorrow's revolutionaries. Dr Coleman offers an understanding of the society we live in, in order to show where our freedom was lost.*'
(Greenock Telegraph)

Paperback £12.99
Published by EMJ Books
Order from Publishing House • Trinity Place • Barnstaple • Devon EX32 9HG • England
Telephone 01271 328892 • Fax 01271 328768
www.vernoncoleman.com